Foucault

Gilles Deleuze

Translated and edited by
SEÁN HAND

Foreword by
PAUL BOVÉ

University of Minnesota Press
Minneapolis   London

Originally published in French © 1986 by
Les Éditions de Minuit.

Published by the University of Minnesota Press
2037 University Avenue Southeast, Minneapolis MN 55414.
Printed in the United States of America on acid-free paper

Third printing, 1992

Library of Congress Cataloging-in-Publication Data

Deleuze, Gilles.
   [Foucault. English]
   Foucault/Gilles Deleuze; translated and edited by Seán Hand.
      p.   cm.
   Includes index.
   ISBN 0–8166–1674–4   ISBN 0–8166–1675–2   (pbk.)
   1. Foucault. Michel.   I. Hand, Seán. II. Title.
B2430.F724D4513 1988
194 - - dc 19   87–31668
                                                             CIP

The University of Minnesota
is an equal-opportunity
educator and employer.

Contents

Foreword: The Foucault Phenomenon: the Problematics
of Style *Paul Bové*   vii

Translating Theory, or the Difference between Deleuze
and Foucault [Translator's Introduction]   xli

Acknowledgements   xlv

Abbreviations   xlvii

From the Archive to the Diagram

A New Archivist (*The Archaeology of Knowledge*)   1

A New Cartographer (*Discipline and Punish*)   23

Topology: 'Thinking Otherwise'

Strata or Historical Formations: the Visible and
the Articulable (Knowledge)   47

Strategies or the Non-stratified:
the Thought of the Outside (Power)   70

Foldings, or the Inside of Thought (Subjectivation)   94

Appendix: On the Death of Man and Superman   124

Notes   133

Index   155

Foreword
The Foucault Phenomenon:
the Problematics of Style
Paul A. Bové

"The aim of critique is not the ends of man or of reason but in the end the Overman, the overcome, over-
taken man. Ths point of critique is not justification
but a different way of feeling: another sensibility."

Gilles Deleuze, *Nietzsche and Philosophy*

"But, after all, this was the proper task of a history
of thought, as against a history of behaviors or
representations: to define the conditions in which human beings 'problematize' what they are, what they
do, and the world in which they live."

Michel Foucault, *The Uses of Pleasure*

"Would Zarathustra steal this bite from the devil?
Well then, we wish you a good meal."

Friedrich Nietzsche, *Thus Spake Zarathustra*

I

Many of Foucault's most telling statements—often some of his
weakest and most controversial—come in interviews and occasional essays. They often occur in an admonitory mode when he

tries to correct the very self-interested images of him and his work that scholars create in line with their own intellectual, political, and professional needs. Because there is commonly such a buzz of contradictory comment going on around him — as his friends and enemies push him to the left, right, and center or sometimes off the political spectrum altogether — Foucault could assert that it proves what he contends: conventional categories really don't fit him; he is posing an entirely new and different set of questions about a whole range of sometimes unthought of matters.[1] Since his early death in 1984, that left so many of his projects incomplete, the academic effort to appropriate, correct, or dismiss Foucault has gone on even more intensely — sometimes brilliantly,[2] sometimes stupidly,[3] and sometimes with troubling seriousness.[4]

The Foucault debate is so profitable that it has a peculiar academic allure. It attracts the attention of anyone who hopes to consider Foucault and tempts him or her to write an essay instead about the ongoing conversation: where so many renowned Professors gather to argue, there is an air of excitement, energy, and significance that draws one with its promise of pleasure, stimulation, and reward.

One of my interests in this foreword is to analyze some parts of the structure of reception that incorporates Foucault into North American academic intellectual circles — especially Philosophy and Literary Criticism — both to get some insight into the apparatus underlying those structures and to preserve some of Foucault's originary value as a critical alternative to them. Moreover, it seems to me, examining how these academic circles function in dealing with Foucault, whose own work is so forcefully critical of their knowledge politics, will provide a privileged insight into some aspects of these structures' workings while reclaiming something of the originary critical force of Foucault's work — a force that, as I hope to show, these structures function to dissipate.[5]

Of course, an introduction to a book *on* Foucault, especially a translation of one written by Gilles Deleuze, Foucault's ally and friend, unavoidably must say something about the place and position that book occupies in the Foucault debate, and one can take the occasion of its appearance to comment on and worry about the system of reception that awaits it. One can easily see that Deleuze's is the best study of Foucault to date. He treats Foucault in a style and within a problematic that, while not Foucault's own, contrast favorably with the efforts both of analytically trained philosophers to represent Foucault in the incongruously alien style of their professional discourse and the ways in which significant elements of literary criticism — on the "Left" and "Right" — have appropriated and resisted him.[6]

For example, and by way of contrast with Deleuze, I would like to consider Charles Taylor's extremely careful explication and critique "Foucault on Freedom and Truth," which follows the path taken recently by powerful thinkers such as Habermas and Nancy Fraser[7] in trying to oblige Foucault to answer questions about issues raised within the very systems of discourse that, as Foucault himself put it once, come from the very "mind-set" he was trying to critique. (A bit further on in the essay, I shall turn to the writings of Fredric Jameson to offer an analysis not of the "entire" genealogy of such a complex intellectual but of some effects of the political knowledge-apparatus at work in the North American reception of Foucault — precisely as these appear in even such a historically aware dialectical thinker as Jameson.)

Taylor's essay is worth commenting on because it is more extended than Habermas's treatment of Foucault and develops aspects of Nancy Fraser's position (although without noting her essay). Also, Taylor is an eminent philosopher often identified as sympathetic with continental traditions in a way many of his colleagues (those who take a stand against the "pluralist" rebels within the APA) are not. Furthermore, Taylor is a politicized intellectual often spoken of admirably for his "organic" connection to resisting elements in Canadian society. For these reasons his politically "left" and philosophically "open" attitude make him an important limit case for understanding how and to what ends analytically trained Professors of Philosophy can represent Foucault. My point about Taylor cannot be made easily by a brief quotation, but perhaps the problem can be suggested by his nearly final remark that with Foucault's last step toward "acknowledging" his own "sources" "the really interesting debate can begin, on the issues which count, which *Foucault's mode of expression up to now has obscured*" (CT, 99: my emphasis).

That Taylor then goes on to identify the two "issues which count" is less interesting than what the italicized part of his remark suggests. His essay proceeds by allegorizing Foucault's texts, by "telling stories," as the analytic philosophers like to say, or, perhaps more accurately, by rephrasing the "stories" about power, man, history, truth, etc., he feels he finds embedded within Foucault's work. He rephrases Foucault's writings so that he can consider them in light of the "history" of philosophical discussion of those questions. But Taylor has set himself what he must consider a difficult task because, as he sees it, Foucault's style "obscures" his stories. Taylor's practical, methodological, disciplinary response to this difficulty is not hard to sketch. He paraphrases or quotes Foucault and then rephrases the "position" he feels he has found badly enunciated there. As Taylor would have it, several of these "positions" — once adequately distilled by the analytic philosopher to release their essential point — can be seen to contradict each other as, for example, when we are told that Foucault cannot hold the "position" he does on "power" and "truth": " 'Power' without 'freedom' or 'truth': can there really be an analysis which raises *the notion of power*, and which leaves no place for freedom, or truth?" (CT, p. 90). There is no point to debating Taylor's "reading" of Foucault. Given Taylor's aims and the disciplinary burdens inscribed within his techniques — the effects of which quite precisely are to produce such comments — a serious debate, one that raised the question of determining forces as such, could not be carried out. Such a debate would inevitably have to come to the point of asking Taylor to examine critically — and that means here historically, politically, and genealogically — the value of his discipline's values. It would mean, rather obviously, taking up the kind of critique carried out by Nietzsche in *On The Genealogy of Morals* and extended by Foucault to matters of institutions, politics, and knowledge-production. But, as I shall try to show, these are precisely among the very questions it is Taylor's disciplinary function to deflect — despite his sympathies for European Philosophy and his presumed status as an "organic intellectual." What we have, then, when we read Taylor on Foucault is a doubled appearance: he seems to be trying simply to clarify Foucault for our benefit; but this points to another appearance: he is writing Foucault into the discourse of analytic Philosophy and so making him more available for discussion and correction. This last makes Taylor vulnerable to a critique that suspects the disciplinary status of Philosophy, to the kind of work done, for example, by Richard Rorty in *Philosophy and the Mirror of Nature*.[8] From this point of view, Taylor appears simply as a good Philosophical worker: presenting more adequate, consistent, and empirically defensible stories about these traditional matters in a way that lets Philosophers "recognize" them, that is, "recollect" them in the Kierkegaardian sense: "for what is recollected has been, is repeated backwards."[9] The "recollection" takes place by giving Foucault "positions" and by assigning him a site where Philosophers can reason about him. This process of institutionalized "recollection" works because it is inscribed within the network of "power/knowledge" that Foucault, following Nietzsche, has limned for us. Taylor's efforts to deal with Foucault must be traced to this level of inscription; following him through the crossings of these networks will show why Foucault has done something meaningful in sketching the power/knowledge apparatus and why many leading humanistic intellectuals misread him: namely, to blunt the political consequences of his critique of their disciplines', their discourses', and their own positions within the knowledge/power apparatus.

Tracing these reflected levels of work means beginning with a critique of the readily apparent in Taylor's reading of Foucault. Within the general procedures of allegorization Taylor employs,[10] one specific instance of Taylor's practice stands out, unsurprisingly, as centrally problematic, namely his discussion of Foucault's famous figure, "the regime of truth." Here is the first passage Taylor quotes:

> Each society has its regime of truth, its "general politics" of truth: that is, the types of discourse which it accepts and makes function as true; the mechanisms and instances which enable one to distinguish true and false statements, the means by which each is sanctioned; the techniques and procedures accorded value in the acquisition of truth; the status of those who are charged with saying what counts as true.[11]

Taylor's comment on this passage is simply: "In this relationship Foucault sees truth as subordinated to power"(CT, p. 93). Such a notion, Taylor paraphrases Foucault as saying, "is even more emphatically so in our society" (CT, p. 93), which leads to Taylor's second citation from Foucault (which I give with Taylor's elisions):

> There can be no possible exercise of power without a certain economy of discourses of truth which operates through and on the basis of this association. We are subjected to the production of truth through power and we cannot exercise power except through the production of truth. This is the case of every society, but I believe that in ours the relationship between power, right, and truth is organized in a highly specific fashion. . . . I would say that we are forced to produce the truth of power that our society demands, of which it has need, in order to function: we *must* speak the truth; we are constrained or condemned to confess to or discover the truth. Power never ceases its interrogation, its inquisition, its registration of truth; it institutionalizes, professionalizes and rewards its pursuit. In the last analysis, we must produce truth as we must produce wealth.[12]

Taylor then offers us a six and one-half line paraphrase of this passage as a "line of thought." "This position," he writes, "is easy enough to state baldly" (CT, p. 94).

What do we see Taylor doing? As he presents it, he cuts through Foucault's obfuscating style and restates his positions clearly and lucidly. He then tests whether these positions are consistent and adequate. His chief concern is whether they "make sense": "I am arguing that power, in his sense, *does not make sense* without at least the idea of liberation" (CT, p. 92). Foucault's idea of the "regime-relativity of truth" is "difficult — or impossible — actually to integrate with the logic of one's analytical discourse" (CT, p. 94). If we are interested in making a second-level disciplinary critique of Taylor on this point, we might say that he has measured Foucault by a certain unannounced and unexamined set of argumentative standards of signification which he thinks are central to "reasoning" itself — whereas we might easily say that they belong rather to the constitutive practice of the discipline of which he is a leading exponent. His remarks would then be seen as wanting: we could say, in language something like his own, that he has failed to put together any demonstrative case that this certain kind of sense must be made before any thought can be found acceptable; furthermore, as he works on Foucault's complex writing, he unspokenly assumes that "sense" itself must be the end of discursive writing and that it must result from an integrated logic of analytic discourse. More interesting, though, we could distance ourselves from Taylor's language and say that he has made no effort to understand the genealogical burden of his discipline, its discourses, its institutional forms, and his place within it. We could then say he knows not what he does. But that would be to accuse him of not having done the impossible: taking an ironically and historically critical position on his own disciplinary formation so that he might then self-confidently cut across it all. In other words, it would be to accuse him of not being Nietzsche or Foucault! We must be satisfied, however, with the simpler perception that Taylor has been trained (and come to accept) the premium placed by his discipline upon a certain kind of thought (on this Deleuze will clarify a great deal; see pp. 77ff.) that can only proceed along certain expected lines of argumentation. (It should be noted that I am not saying that this alone determines Taylor's reading or the limits of his critique.) We can see, then, that one tactic is fundamental to Taylor's practice throughout this essay; and we might speculate that perhaps it is a disciplinary characteristic: the reduction of Foucault's text, of his style and writing to "position." We must be clear that Taylor's notion of "position" is not the same as the poststructuralist figure of "positionality" which represents the effort to describe the historical, textual topology of argument, power, and interconnections within or across overdetermined intellectual and discursive productions. For Taylor, "one's position" seems to mean just a "set of ideas" or an idea that one holds and tries to defend (often obscurely) by writing "arguments" or "telling stories" in an essay or book or collection of essays and/or books. I want to suggest that it is naïve for Taylor to approach the text of a leading theoretician of writing, language, literature, and style as if his writing were merely a failed attempt at transparently presenting "positions," something merely unfortunately "obscure." It is especially ineffective, or naïve, when the writer is Foucault who, perhaps even more than Gramsci, has done much to rethink, to problematize, the role of the intellectual and the relations between power and the practice of discourses and disciplines.

Perhaps we are now in a position to conclude that Taylor seems guilty of the very "crime" with which he charges Foucault: he tries to stand nowhere, outside history, especially outside the historicity and cultural specificity of his own discipline's discourse and practice. In other words, by not taking his own disciplinary standards under critical historical investigation, he proceeds as if they were, as if he were—at least as a Professor of Philosophy—outside the reach of historical and political determinations.

We can see this in the "intent" and "content" of Taylor's essay: he wants to offer a more "adequate" left-liberal political theory than Foucault's and to do so must assume that we have progressed in truth (CT, p. 97). Not only does he make the expected assertion that evidence for this progress can be found in the history of the natural sciences, but he makes the very revelatory remark that such progress can also be found in the philosophical discourse which follows, explicates, and legitimates scientific and other "truths." What is interesting about this remark is the authority it claims for analytic Philosophy, especially as this is derived from its apparently secondary function of legitimating scientific truth—which now appears as the first condition of its own institutional legitimacy—and from its emulation of scientific standards. It is the kind of remark that, if we continue with our second-level critique, we might say gives the game away. In turn we would urge Taylor to take seriously, as all too many of his colleagues have not, Rorty's valuable dramatization of "Philosophy's" status as a professional discipline and discourse.[13]

More interesting for our purposes rather than for this second-level critique would be a reading of this remark as a trace of Taylor's wish not to think seriously about the implications of the "regime of truth" for professional philosophical practice. How can we read his remark in this way? By reading across Foucault's text, not with an eye to paraphrasing the "connative" elements alone, but with a desire to see something of how Foucault's texts work within the power/knowledge apparatus of intellectual discourse. If we re-examine the lecture of 14 January 1976 (from which Taylor draws the second of his extended quotations), we rediscover that it was a central part of Foucault's effort to replace the traditional philosophical "question" about truth fixing limits "to the rights of power" with different and more specific ones: "what rules of right are implemented by the relations of power in the production of discourses of truth? . . . what type of power is susceptible of producing dimensions of truth that in a society such as ours are endowed with such potent effects?"[14] These questions precede and position the passages Taylor quotes — and it is significant that Taylor does not choose to begin his commentary with them. In other words, with his emphatic concern for internal consistency of analytic discourse and his explicatory technique of reductive paraphrase, Taylor exemplifies and embodies both the traditional philosophical question Foucault decries as problematic and the use of an unreflected but nonetheless empowered "discourse of truth": the aim, to establish once more "reason's" rights in setting the limits of power within thought and culture — but now with "reason" circumscribed within the institutionalized forms of Philosophy legitimated by the assured progress of truth.

More specifically, Taylor, whom, we must remember, some would see as an "organic intellectual" given his non-academic concerns with labor in Canada, appears in his "professional" work as a "traditional intellectual," in Gramsci's sense;[15] he appears as a "free-floating cosmopolitan" in his clerical and fraternal commitment to timeless questions of "truth" as understood according to de-historicized standards of rational consistency. His comments on the figure of the "regime of truth" trope defensively against Foucault's genealogical critiques of intellectual practice in the face of new forms of institutional politics. Taylor's defensive moves represent the traditional intellectual's resistance both to his[16] historical belatedness and, somewhat paradoxically, to recognizing his own professionally and hence politically conservative function — precisely *as* a traditional intellectual. Furthermore, his rhetoric and practice turn against the very claim that there is political value in discussing the "regime of truth" and in marking genealogically the places of intellectual discourses within the apparatuses of power/knowledge that Foucault has helped us discern at work in the organization of culture and society.[17]

Foucault's presentation of "the regime of truth" follows immediately upon his statement "that we are now at a point where the function of the specific intellectual needs to be reconsidered. Reconsidered but not abandoned, despite the nostalgia of some for the great 'universal' Intellectuals."[18] For Foucault, the "regime of truth" cannot be represented without tracing, among other things, the position and function of the intellectual "politically in his specific relation to a local form of power."[19] Foucault's analysis of "intellectuals" does not represent them traditionally in terms of "expertise," "State service," or "ideology." Rather, he tropes on these figures so that they have a new theoretical and political utility: the masses know, for example, that they are implicated in the social effects of "expertise"; "State service" comes to reveal the intellectual's strategic position, often within the extended state, often as part of non-state hegemonic institutions; and the reproduction and redistribution of "ideology" is secondary to the fundamental matter, namely, "the effects proper to true discourse."[20] Not surprisingly, Taylor's comments selectively skirt this issue to reduce Foucault's concerns on these matters to the slogan "Foucault sees truth as subordinated to power" (CT, p. 93) — despite the fact that in the very words immediately preceding the one sentence Taylor quotes, Foucault has written: "it [truth] induces regular effects of power."[21]

Although these concerns occupy a central place in Foucault's practice, Taylor nowhere explicitly raises the issues of the intellectuals' relations to power or the State, nor does he bother with the genealogy of "truth," except to say that such concerns as these, if followed out, bring one to the untenable Nietzschean conclusions of relativism and perspectivism. What is one to say about these strange omissions in a reading of Foucault? What is being avoided? One can only conclude that it is the role and fate of the intellectual that Taylor cannot consider, that he permanently turns against. Given the texts he has chosen to paraphrase, one can assume that it is the figure of the "specific intellectual" Taylor recognizes as challenging both his left-liberal assumptions and goals and his position within the "regime of truth" as a "traditional intellectual." But refusing to engage with the figure of the specific intellectual is an *aggressively* defensive move. Insofar as this figure is Foucault's own partial self-representation, a representation of the critical genealogical intellectual's struggle within and against the empowered and empowering dominant discourses, its erasure is Foucault's erasure. Of course, such an assertion depends upon a full reading of Foucault's work as an attempt genealogically to cast in relief the positivities of power/knowledge in forming the dominant regime of truth and to theorize the illegitimacy of the important discursive practices and nondiscursive institutions central to that very regime.

Such a reading would give a central place to the intellectual, both as a key to Foucault's critique of the history of the present and as a central element in his theorizing an alternative politics and sense of "truth." Taylor's aggressive defense then occludes Foucault's discussion of the intellectual because of its power to destabilize the very operations of the power/knowledge apparatus Taylor's work defends and in which it participates. Were it successful, this occlusion would blot out the resistance of Foucault's work to being inscribed within networks of discourse and discipline that embody and exemplify the regime of truth it challenges.

In a literary context, we might put the matter simply: Taylor has no critical sympathy; it is ironic, given the focus of his work, that his error takes the immediate form of hermeneutic blindness; he does not begin his critique by trying to "understand" Foucault in his own terms;[22] rather, he arraigns Foucault before a rigged court that has prejudged him.[23] I use this juridical metaphor to suggest how Taylor remains a high intellectual, linked to liberal forms of power and ideology, occupying a leading position within a formed discipline essential to the existence of the state consensus in Western "democracies." I am suggesting, in other words, that Taylor exemplifies just the link between the grand humanistic intellectual and the liberal state that Foucault begins to elaborate.[24]

It is one of the ironies of hermeneutic blindness that its victim can best be described in his own words: having failed to historicize the discourses and practice of his profession as a Professor of Philosophy, he accuses Foucault of forgetting history:

> We have a *history*. We live in time not just self-enclosed in the present, but essentially related to a past which has helped define our identity, and a future which puts it again into question. (CT, p. 98)

But Taylor writes having forgotten that this is true of all intellectuals and their disciplined discourses; this remains unthought because his practice and its values could not occupy the same strategic position they do in relation to the regime of truth (or the extended state) were he to historicize them and treat them genealogically. The effect is that he sounds as if, as a Philosophy Professor, "he could stand nowhere" (CT, p. 98).

The kinds of self-defensive but aggressively blind moves Taylor makes in this stylistically lucid performance typify the response of "traditional intellectuals" to the problematics Foucault raises. They cannot confront their actual *specificity* in regard to truth's relations with power — cannot in that, as we learn from examining other institutions and discourses more broadly,[25] part of their efficacy rests upon successfully blocking access to the past, making investigations into their genealogy seem unnatural, and empowering alternative and always ahistorical practices as their means of reproduction. The work of critical genealogists like Foucault and Nietzsche delimits the intellectuals' dreams of truth's control of power. As a result, when leading intellectuals of the dominant discourses confront such a critical figure they experience a form of anxiety or stress that leads them to defensive moves. And these moves often take the form of assuring, even "sympathetic," incorporations of these disturbing works — on the model of Foucault's analyses in his study of madness. (Other less subtle but powerful dismissals of these works also occur, but they are less interesting, less dangerous, and less significant for their obvious hostility.[26])

Of course, it is not just Foucault's or Nietzsche's work that is so attacked, but all criticism that challenges the dominance of the hegemonic disciplines and their political and cultural roles.[27] One can say polemically that the established disciplines have their place in the American national project of cultural, racial, and regional dedifferentiation. To consider Foucault, for example, in "established terms" is not only to blunt any awareness of how different his project might be from that carried out by liberal Philosophers, but also to deny the value of his work to others themselves variously engaged in their own struggles within and, if you will, "against" the "regime of truth's" effects on their lives, their identities, and their social positions. Not only "leading figures" but "secondary intellectuals" as well play a role in this process of dedifferentiation.[28] They have at their often unconscious disposal an entire range of ascetic and nihilistic tactics to try to empty these critical impulses of both their negative and futural possibilities.[29] In effect, then, Taylor's comment on Foucault makes him irrelevant to Anglo-American Professors of Philosophy and, more important, to the mainstream of political theory and practice — which thereby preserves its own authority and values and the values upon which those values and that authority rest. In other words, by "recollecting" Foucault into the analytically defined set of "traditional" Philosophical questions and by seeing him as a failure in those terms, Foucault can be dismissed by the discipline that now claims the name of Philosophy. Once Taylor has gotten through Foucault's "unfortunately obscure prose" to the heretofore invisible important issues, Foucault can be left behind by those concerned with "Freedom and Truth."

II

Although I have directed my remarks about Taylor primarily at the critical limits of Philosophy's professional apparatus, I am not suggesting that other disciplinary formations escape implication in this problematic of reception. I especially do not exempt literary criticism, even though I have occasionally used its techniques to critique Taylor. Literary criticism, we should not forget, played a major role in Foucault's "reception" before Philosophy became interested in his work.

Just as I do not think one can find this problematic restricted to one discipline, I do not believe one can identify it as a problem only of the "political right." The "left," especially the Marxist Left, cannot easily develop a self-critical moment out of its encounter with Foucault.[30] There has been considerable hostile ideological debate between "poststructuralists" and "Marxists" that has often resulted in the dismissal of Derrida and Foucault, especially, as idealists and conservative. At times, as in the work of Barry Smart and Cornel West, there have been attempts to engage critically and, up to certain limits, sympathetically with Foucault. Perry Anderson, surely one of the Marxist intellectuals most hostile to poststructuralism, has written an extremely antagonistic and representative critique of Foucault. Anderson develops his thought in an extended comparison of Foucault and Lévi-Strauss:

> A massive analytic machinery is mounted, whose essential goal is to demonstrate the *identity* of the field in question — the invariant function of totems or structure of myths, the unity of epistemes or the rigidity of discursive formations. Once constructed, however, these leave no epistemological passage to the *diversity* of specific myths or enunciations, still less to the *de-*

velopment from one to another. The result is that instead of genuine explanation, structuralist analysis constantly tends to tilt towards classification: "adjacency" as Edward Said has remarked, eclipses "sequentiality."[31]

It is quite typical of this sort of "Left" critique of Foucault that it does not itself reflect upon such enabling notions as "genuine explanation" or "development." The genealogical reasons for occurrences of critical blindness such as these are too difficult even to sketch at this time. That they can lead sometimes to rather silly remarks one can see in Anderson's objection that Foucault does not provide causal class-based analyses when it is precisely Foucault's point that the questioning of just such categories for the work at hand has the highest critical priority.[32]

Anderson's remarks are of interest not only because they exemplify a certain typical critical blindness (also to be seen in Jameson as I shall show subsequently), but also because they suggest, I think uniquely, something of the importance of professional intellectual practice in the development of politically contested and contestatory theories. Anderson, like many others, remarks on the role played by the events of May 1968 in the development of poststructuralism and the turn of French oppositional culture away from the Marxist tradition. But his analysis of this very substantial problem shows something of how the changes within French intellectual institutions and their place in the national political culture must be seen as very important to any understanding of the movement "away from Marx." In other words, Anderson points out the necessity of doing some sort of critical intellectual history in the analysis of emergent theories — but, needless to say, he does not do any of his own position: he does not follow up on another insight to be found in Said, namely the latter's citation of Gramsci's remark that the intellectual must do an "inventory" of himself.[33] That is to say, Anderson has a critical blindness not unlike Taylor's despite his own thematized use of intellectual, institutional history as a way of dismissing Foucault. Like Taylor, and as I shall suggest, like Jameson, Anderson obscures Foucault's work precisely at the moment when a critically sympathetic engagement with it would most threaten him and his "proper" ideological, discursive, and political position. Stabilizing this position costs Anderson critical openness and the corresponding blindness produces dogmatic posturing.

The critical charge most often made against Fredric Jameson is not dogmatism, but eclecticism. The latter is not, it seems to me, an easily sustainable or well-thought-out complaint since Jameson's work so extensively if sometimes seemingly in a baroque way accretes theoretically and historically. In *The Political Unconscious*,[34] Jameson, while arguing that the recent Nietzschean inspired critiques of the dialectic are "misplaced," tells us that Deleuze and Guattari's attack on Freudianism in *Anti-Oedipus* powerfully reminds us of the need for "an immanent or antitranscendent hermeneutic."[35] (In part, the *Anti-Oedipus's* critique of Freudianism is not unlike that I have made of Taylor.) In fact, for Jameson, their critique spurs his construction of a new hermeneutic:

> *The Anti-Oedipus* . . . quite properly takes as its object not Marxian, but rather Freudian, interpretation, which is characterized as a reduction and a rewriting of the whole rich and random multiple realities of concrete everyday experience into the contained, strategically pre-limited terms of the family narrative. . . . What is denounced is therefore a system of allegorical interpretation in which the data of one narrative line are radically impoverished by their rewriting according to the paradigm of another narrative, which is taken as the former's master code or Ur-narrative and proposed as the ultimate hidden or unconscious *meaning* of the first one.

I have already argued that Taylor unknowingly reduces the complexity of Foucault's text to the defining allegory of professional Philosophy's analytic discipline. In so doing, I have, in one sense, extended the Deleuzian and Jamesonian notion of underlying master narrative in a Foucaultian direction by suggesting that there is a "disciplinary unconscious," an institutional narrative that exists as the condition for the reductive allegorization to "story" and "position" that we have seen in Taylor's work.

Nonetheless, what is more interesting in the context that Jameson's comment opens is his reluctance, at this point,[36] to see an equivalent critique of Marxian hermeneutics in Deleuze's work. This is a surprising blindness given Deleuze's strong and persistent critique of the dialectic from his early work on Nietzsche — a critique that develops into Deleuze's (perhaps too) strong anti-Marxian reading of Foucault in this book (for example, p. 38).

But even this is not what is most interesting about Jameson's maneuver in discussing Deleuze and Guattari. Jameson interprets their anti-interpretive project in such a way that he can see it as "very much" in the same spirit as *The Political Unconscious*, and can also find in it a call for a new hermeneutics. This last is interesting because it embodies Jameson's attempt to subsume all anti-dialectical and anti-interpretive historical and political investigations into his own resolutely dialectical and utopian project. In effect, the result of all anti-dialectical critiques — no matter if they are, in Jameson's eyes Foucaultian, Derridean, Kristevan, or whatever — as well as of all anti-hermeneutical analyses is to increase the demand for a dialectical hermeneutics.

> From our present standpoint, however, the ideal of an immanent analysis of the text, of a dismantling or deconstruction of its parts and a description of its functioning and malfunctioning [this is Jameson's reading of the projects of Deleuze and others], amounts less to a wholesale nullification of all interpretive activity than to a demand for the construction of some new and more adequate, immanent or antitranscendent hermeneutic model, which it will be the task of the following pages to propose.

Jameson adds the following as a footnote to this passage:

> From the present perspective, in other words, Deleuze and Guattari's proposal for *anti*interpretive method (which they call schizo-analysis) can equally well be grasped as a new hermeneutic in its own right. It is striking and noteworthy that most of the antiinterpretive positions enumerated . . . above have felt the need to project new "methods" of this kind: thus, the archeology of knowledge, but also, more recently, the "political technology of the body" (Foucault), "grammatology" and deconstruction (Derrida), "symbolic exchange" (Baudrillard), libidinal economy (Lyotard), and "sémanalyse" (Julia Kristeva).

Taylor, we have said, reduces Foucault's work by rewriting it as a story of the Philosophy profession. Jameson is reductive in a different way. (That he is, is less interesting than how and why even he might be.) Understandably working very hard to preserve the critical or negative moment that under the sign of Marcuse he had elaborated as "Utopia" in *Marxism and Form*,[37] he struggles to negate the "anti-Marxist" critical efforts of structuralism and poststructuralism alike on the grounds that they are totalizing synchronic representations of history and consequently preclude all opposition by theorizing it as an element of the system. Above all, the "apparent similarity" between these non-Marxist "total systems" and the proper Marxist "notion of an all-embracing and all-structuring mode of production" bothers Jameson very much.[38] The former are synchronic and relegate all forms of change to the "merely 'diachronic'" (p. 91). Their authors are, in Jameson's rhetoric, deluded by the cybernetic aura of modernity, that is, they see a world "in which the various elements of social life are *programmed* in some increasingly constricted way" (p. 90; my emphasis).[39] Whatever is non-systemic becomes the "contingent." For the Marxist, however, the alternative is clear, as the following extended comment suggests:

> This theoretical foreboding about the limits of synchronic thought can perhaps be most immediately grasped in the political area, where the model of the "total system" would seem slowly and inexorably to eliminate any possibility of the *negative* as such, and to reintegrate the place of an oppositional or even merely "critical" practice and resistance back into the system as the latter's mere inversion.

One can only support Jameson's call for preserving the possibility of the negative, of critique, in postmodernity. About that there should be no quibble among those who are "oppositional." His fear is that the authors of "total systems" eliminate the negative from culture and politics because, as Habermas would also have it, their work is conservative in essence — in the service of the hegemony by virtue of its very "pessimism." That is, these theoreticians unknowingly serve the hegemony they seemingly intend to critique by making the current world order seem inevitable, unalterable, natural — without a past or future; they close down all real forms of resistance by declaring them non-systemic and so "contingent" and ineffective.

Jameson's position is a remarkably anxious one, and with good reason given the totalizing, naturalizing, and dedifferentiating urges of modernist and postmodernist intellectual political practice from, say, Lukacs to Althusser to Frye. Yet there is a troubling limitation to Jameson's formulation of the threat, as we can see in one of his most powerful rhetorical moves: when he asserts that there can be no critique of his classification of an entire body of "oppositional" work as synchronic, as resulting in "total system" theories. For the ground of any such critique of his claim, Jameson asserts, would have to be one of those very systems he has already defined as "synchronic" and therefore as inimicable both to negation and opposition. In other words, Jameson's anxiety is about identity and propriety: anxious to differentiate the "synchronic" from the Marxist, the legitimately authorized intellectual from the usurping conservative and nihilist pretenders, his text stops its own critical dialectic in a way that reveals the workings of academic power upon the limits of oppositional theory and practice. As I have suggested, we can perhaps best locate Jameson's anxiety in the pre-emptive strike he attempts against those he identifies as his opponents:

> in the framework of the analysis of culture also, the latter's integration into a synchronic model would seem to empty cultural production of all its antisystemic capacities, and to "unmask" even the works of an overtly oppositional or political stance as instruments ultimately *programmed* by the system itself. (p. 91; my emphasis)

That is to say, Jameson effectively positions any analysis that places the work of the (non-dialectical) politically or culturally "oppositional" within the effective reach of the ruling order in such a way that its critical force, its negativity, can be dismissed in advance. How so? By reducing the complex critical analysis of the effects of operating as an oppositional figure within hegemonic discourses and institutions to an "unmasking," and, presumably, to a dismissal of their value. Having postulated out of his anxiety ("a number of theorists have been disturbed by the apparent convergence" [p. 91]) a monolithic figure of the "total systemizers," *he* has left open no possibility for the subtle and historically nuanced critique of such positions as his own — even in the name of the complex texture of everyday life in diachrony that he rightly values. He has gotten himself into a position he cannot really desire, a position where one would find it hard to take seriously, for example, Benjamin's reminder that *every* monument of civilization is also a marker of barbarism. That is, even the most powerful politically oppositional practices and theories of Marx and Lenin, for instance, cannot escape the historical reality of their own dialectical position, of their own contradictions, if you will. Of course, Jameson knows this,[40] but this line of thought does not bring him to the point of rethinking the anxiety that leads him to the false binary opposition of "total system" and "totality." Or for want of a more convenient slogan, the exaggerated and unnuanced figure that opposes "Marx" to "Foucault." Rather it gets subsumed into a defensive maneuver by means of which he "unmasks" the "totalizers" so as to deny them both their complexity — even, if you will, their dialectical, historical, contradictory position — and their potential for "critiquing," for doing any "unmasking" of their own.[41] In sum, what we have here is an unannounced struggle for intellectual priority and authority that is hermeneutically violent and a too-abrupt determination that the "negative" can be at work in a complex modern or postmodern society within only one form of critical intellectual, oppositional practice. That this must be the case despite Jameson's commitment to the master-narrative of the struggle between Freedom and Necessity makes the limit we have seen to dialectical thinking only the more sad.

III

Essentially, Jameson has misread Foucault according to the rule of professional intellectual anxiety within the current rapidly changing political situation: one must resist the analysis that suspects the oppositional intellectual's work of being marked by the disciplines and institutions in which she or he labors. That we can see Jameson reflected in this law — even so distantly — is a sign of its power, especially given Jameson's own early, formative, and influential insistence (in *Marxism and Form*) upon the need dialectically to reflect upon the subject's position in the processes of thought. Perhaps, however, the limitation occurs in Jameson because he has not been suspicious enough of the discursive effects of institutionalized disciplines. In any event, the result is the politically motivated, too hasty dismissal of Foucault at the cost of what he has to teach us about the position of intellectuals within power.

Deleuze's Foucault is entirely different from Jameson's or Taylor's. Jameson, we recall, worried that Foucault's "totalizing" thought would close down social spaces in which opposition to the dominant present might develop. Such a worry is misplaced when one remembers how extensive is Foucault's effort to contest the ruling systems of knowledge production as in itself a condition for the possibility of precisely such "negation," just such openings toward a future. Deleuze, discussing Foucault's use of the diagram, puts the matter succinctly and effectively:

> It makes history by unmaking preceding realities and significations, constituting hundreds of points of emergence or creativity, unexpected conjunctions or improbable continuums. It doubles history with a sense of continual evolution. (p. 35)

Several of the themes that go to make up Deleuze's image of Foucault intersect on this matter of the future, of a becoming: the double (*doublure*), the State, the Party, the Outside, the machine. Implicitly it rests upon a rejection of Jameson and others' too simplistic assertion, one that has now unfortunately widely come to be taken as true, that in Foucault's work "power" is a totalizing and homogenizing concept that dedifferentiates the particularities of power in regard to class. Deleuze, it seems to me, rightly insists that for Foucault, "in brief, power is not homogeneous but can be defined only by the particular points through which it passes" (p. 25). It is precisely in Foucault's developed sense of singularity that we find a new notion of the local: the "local" comes to be opposed to the "global" or the "total system" not because it refers only to a particular and identifiable point, for example, the training of bodies in schools; but precisely because it opposes to the global system the notion of power as diffuse and diffused. In other words, it constitutes a way to think the relations of power without either detaching each "instance," as it were, from its interwoven and overdetermined relationships, or moving toward a model of the "total system." Indeed, it can displace as well the Sartrean notion of the "project" as Jameson develops it in regard to the "totality."[42] Foucault's insight is part of what Deleuze calls a "new functionalism":

Foucault's functionalism throws up a new topology which no longer locates the origin of power in a privileged place, and can no longer accept a limited localization. . . . Here we can see that 'local' has two very different meanings: power is local because it is never global, but it is not local or localized because it is diffuse. (p. 26)

Deleuze's reading of Foucault's figure of the "local" as the diffuse and diffused is of real importance since it gives a critical edge to Foucault's notion of the "specific intellectual" engaged in guerilla warfare against the empowered and dominant system of knowledge production. "Power effects" need to be diagrammed not because there is any hope of developing a totalizing picture of the relations of force in a culture or economy — that is, there is no synchronic dream here — but precisely because they cannot be embraced by any concept or mode of thought that sets itself up as their expansive equivalent. In other words, the essentially Gramscian notion that capital and the state can only be opposed by a war of position, by adopting a strategy of opposition that can be effective only as long as its own reach is, as it were, as extensive as that of its opponent's lines — this notion cannot by itself serve as an adequate guide to opposition since, in effect, it insists upon inscribing itself as a reflection of what it hopes to negate or transcend. Furthermore, it is a model historically embedded in an earlier formation, one that is liberal or modernist, one that is mechanical, and so, even in its own terms, is an inadequate reflection of the dispersed and unequal effects of power within late capitalist societies and between them and postcolonial cultures. Finally, the notion of "strategic opposition" forces even as subtle a dialectician as Jameson (or as professional an oppositional intellectual as Edward W. Said)[43] to a moment of critical blindness that results from and also develops into an unwillingness to consider the relationships of oppositional practice to the institutionalized forms of discourse through which the dominant forms of power/knowledge sometimes have constitutive as well as limiting effects. It is just because one realizes after Foucault that one cannot think to have identified power in a locale that one is most likely to be suspicious of one's own inscription within the power/knowledge apparatus at the moment when one is developing the most powerful or authoritative of critical or oppositional instruments. This is not to say, of course, that such an awareness blunts the effects and values of these instruments; but it does mean that one must constantly use these tools with a sharp eye out for that moment when the limit of their utility is reached. It is a limit always present, "in the final analysis," but not a limit always present, in each moment, as it were, as it would be if one were thinking of it as a matter of dialectical contradiction. Rather, the limit arrives in a way analogous to what R. P. Blackmur describes as the failure of a symbol, as the breakdown from excess of a congery of words that has come to have collective value, but finally and beneficially fails from overload—from its coming up against its inevitable inscription in the existing power/knowledge system, or, as Blackmur might put it, the present form of a burdensome but useful tradition.[44]

Deleuze's book brilliantly explores the theoretical, figurative, and political implications of this notion. He expands upon his own earlier work on Nietzsche in such a way that we understand how some of Foucault's characteristic concerns with the "double," the notion of the "outside," and the *enoncé* come from a style of thinking—not to be confused, as Deleuze shows, with "reason" or "philosophy"—and a style of writing that tactically resists the reification of critical inventions. As Deleuze puts it apropos of Foucault's own theoretical reflection on this process: "If the fold and unfold animate not only Foucault's ideas but even his style, it is because they constitute an archaeology of thought" (p. 129). We can see Deleuze tracing this archaeology to its beginnings in Foucault's reading of biology's origins—where the "fold" and "unfold" are figures consistent with the diffusion of power as the local. Both Cuvier and Saint-Hilaire invoke the "fold": one as a third dimension that makes impossible a surface passage from one type to another; the other as a third dimension opening up deeper passages. More politically, as Deleuze reads Foucault, in modernity actions such as work lose their association with the qualities and orders that had elevated them to infinity. The diffusion of power separates them from these qualities and hollows them out as something that becomes unqualifiable, impossible to represent; they become death in life—pain and fatigue in work, stammering or aphasia in language. Even the earth, Deleuze says, discovers its avarice and loses its apparent order of infinity (cf. p. 126ff.).

Deleuze makes much of Foucault's antistatism, of what Baudrillard feels results in anarchism.[45] Much has already been written — favorably and unfavorably — about this matter; Jameson, for example, accepts Baudrillard's claim that Foucault's position leaves us in a situation where anarchism, terrorism, or other forms of disorganized and useless kinds of protest are all that is possible.[46] But Deleuze emphasizes that Foucault's sense of the diffusion of power is a challenge not only to Statist theories but also to theories of the oppositional or vanguard Party.

Deleuze reads Foucault's figure of the Outside as involving "the pure transmission of unique elements which remain points of indetermination, since they are not yet defined and limited by the curve of the statement that joins them up" (p. 11). What is emitted is, as it were, the enoncé; and the Outside is the possibility of the iteration of the enoncé. "A statement is in itself a repetition" (p. 12). What it repeats may be something that is seemingly identical and strange and identical in its strangeness. For Deleuze, this repetition has revolutionary potential: referring to the end of *Archeology of Knowledge*, he wonders what this might be if not Foucault's call for a general theory of production that may be elided with a revolutionary practice, revolutionary in its invention or discovery of the fact that discourse takes its form in the element of an "Outside" that is indifferent to my life and my death. For Deleuze an inevitable opposition to Marxism follows from this insight into the Outside. What Foucault develops from it is a new functionalism that is not class-based analysis, but addresses a "new tableau." In other words, Deleuze discovers a homology between the singularity of the enoncés and the nature of power: "In brief, power is not homogeneous but can be defined only by the particular points through which it passes" (p. 25). For Foucault, then, the State is an effect of power, the effect of the assembled forces of governmentality placed on another level.

It follows, as Deleuze shows us, that Foucault's challenge to the centrality of the State results in a challenge to the Party: the theoretical privilege given to the State as the apparatus of power has consequent upon it — by virtue of the logic of reflection — a sense of the party as director, centralizer — as leading ultimately to the conquest of State power. Deleuze tells us that Foucault's theories bring us to another conception of the Party — but he does not tell us what this might be! In fact, one must think that Deleuze has made an error here for it seems incredible that Foucault would have welcomed the notion of a new Party at all. Given Foucault's enormous suspicion of institutions and his sense of their role in political relations of knowledge and authority, one can only assume that Deleuze would himself like to have an alternate conception, would like to have a Party again.

Foucault theorizes the State and the Party as he theorizes other institutions, and his aim is to do so in a style that exceeds the grasp of the "regime of truth." His thought insists upon the instability of the rapport of forces that define any strategic milieu; as such, "power" is, as Deleuze insists, an informal or unformed concept: "power" passes through points that are singular and not formed (cf. p. 73). Given, then, that power is diffuse and unformed, and that the concept "power" is equally unformed and informal, the question arises how one can think this theoretically irreducible figure. Foucault invents the category of the "micro-physics of power" to do just that. Deleuze cautions that a micro-physics must not be imagined as a miniaturization of visible or enunciable forms, but as another domain, a new type of relations, a dimension of thought irreducible to knowledge: mobile and non-localizable relationships (cf pp. 73–74). Using this figure of the "micro-physics of power" shapes Foucault's discussion of institutions, including the State and the Party. They are not and cannot be the source or essence of power. Indeed, they have neither essence nor interiority. Simply, they reproduce the relations of force that sustain them. The State like all other organizations simply organizes the supposed relationships (p. 76) of governmental power and these forces are microphysical. For Foucault, institutions have two roles and facets: they have apparatuses and rules: they organize, in effect, the grand visibilities, the field of visibility, and the grand narratives, the regime of the enoncés.

Deleuze does not long rest with this critical notion of the microphysics of power, with its effect of negating the regime of truth. To understand why not, we should recall that in *Nietzsche and Philosophy*,[47] Deleuze reads the notion of the eternal return in such a way that it becomes the transcendence of the negative: "The eternal return transmutes the negative: it turns the heavy into something light" (p. 86). What is attractive about this moment in Deleuze is the return of the affirmative, the positive in the destructive moment that is critique.[48] Deleuze continues his thought on the eternal recurrence by saying "it makes negation a power of affirming." That is, as Deleuze goes on in a tone that suggests both Heidegger and, interestingly, Walter Benjamin,[49] "negation in this new form has become critique: destruction becomes active, aggression profoundly linked to affirmation. Critique is destruction as joy, the aggression of the creator. The creator of values cannot be distinguished from a destroyer, from a criminal, or from a critic: a critic of established values, reactive values and baseness" (p. 87). The source of this insight is Zarathustra's Prologue, as Deleuze tells us in a later note: "Z Prologue 9: 'the destroyer, the criminal — but he is the creator'; Z I 15 'whoever creates must always destroy.' "(p. 208, n. 14)

Deleuze recasts this aesthetic and somewhat metaphysical notion in his figuration of Foucault in which he represents Foucault as showing that critical practice, or "destruction," requires cutting transverse lines across the field of power/knowledge. This, Deleuze says, is "thinking." He sees Foucault following Heidegger only to a certain point in this notion of "thinking," but developing more fundamentally a Nietzschean insight that commits the thinker to the prophecy of the future:

> The inside condenses the past (a long period of time) in ways that are not at all continuous but instead confront it with a future that comes from outside, exchange it and re-create it. To think means to be embedded in the present-time stratum that serves as a limit: what can I see and what can I say today? But this involves thinking of the past as it is condensed in the inside, in the relation to oneself. . . . We will then think the past against the present and resist the latter, not in favour of a return but 'in favour, I hope, of a time to come' (Nietzsche), that is, by making the past active and present to the outside so that something new will finally come about, so that thinking, always, may reach thought. Thought thinks its own history (the past), but in order to free itself from what it thinks (the present) and be able finally to 'think otherwise' (the future). (pp. 119–20)

Placing him within this prophetic sense of time not only links Foucault to Heidegger (especially the latter's concept of the three ecstasies) and to Benjamin (especially on memory and the story-teller), but also provides something of a Nietzschean response to the charges leveled by Habermas and others that Foucault has "unannounced norms": the prophet has no normative values as the Philosopher understands them; rather he has what we might call a severe utopian vision that projects into the future even when there is no alternative world imagined in that vision.

To associate Foucault with some prophetic visionary capacity such as this is, I think, Deleuze's aim. He would have it that Foucault attempts to gain a transcendent and metaphysical overview of the knowledge/power apparatus while suspended above the cracks between enoncés and visibilities:

> But at the same time we try to climb above the strata in order to reach an outside, an atmospheric element, a "non-stratified substance" that would be capable of explaining how the two forms of knowledge can embrace and intertwine on each stratum, from one edge of the fissure to the other. (p. 121)

One cannot but feel a metaphysical tinge in this position, this assigning of visionary power to a subject able to survey the "cracks" between discontinuities. In fact, it seems unavoidably to create a privileged subject of Foucault, a fact hard to reconcile with Foucault's own reservations about the historicity of subject formation and his last books' concern to argue that style is the artistic process that alone can make a life, a subject.

Deleuze's emphasis on this subjective visionary power is perhaps most understandable in light of his intense insistence upon Foucault's anti-Marxism, especially when he insists upon the prophetic visionary power of the transcendent subject as the condition for the revolution he has presented as the potential outcome of Foucault's work. But if Deleuze sees a theory of production in Foucault that can be elided with a revolutionary sense of differential repetition, it appears to be the case that Deleuze thinks this only because his relatively optimistic view of the social, political possibilities inherent in "capitalist evolution" might be unsettling to some. Deleuze correctly sees Foucault as revising Kant on the matter of enlightenment and recovering some of the original impact of critique as Kant himself dampened it. So it is not ironic when Deleuze gets to his crucial political statement by deriving from Foucault a certain Kantian move:

> What is our light and what is our language, that is to say, our "truth" today? What powers must we confront, and what is our capacity for resistance, today when we can no longer be content to say that old struggles are no longer worth anything? And do we not perhaps above all bear witness to and even participate in the "production of a new subjectivity"? Do not the changes in capitalism find an unexpected "encounter" in the slow emergence of a new Self as a centre of resistance? Each time there is a social change [in Capitalism], is there not a movement of subjective reconversion, with its ambiguities but also its potential? These questions may be considered more important than a reference to man's universal rights, including in the realm of pure law. (p. 115)

In other words, Deleuze brings his image of Foucault to a point where the charges of Habermas — that Foucault is a "neo-conservative" — and Jameson — that Foucault makes seemingly "natural" the dominant order — would be more difficult to resist — and these are charges of some importance to the North American discussion of Foucault. What is perhaps most worrying about this is that it makes harder developing the kind of dialogue between Foucault and Gramsci that many scholars have been attempting.[50] More specifically, it turns Foucault's rigorous insistence that he is not a visionary, not an imaginer of the future into a merely formal statement by supposedly revealing the base of Foucault's work to lie, not, as it does, in a severe ascetic critique of the history of the present, but in a utopian impulse raised to a second level of abstraction.[51]

We might say that Deleuze has read Foucault's ironic style with great care and tried to find a way to resist its own constant refusal of the "positive proposition," and of the form of desire that leaves its trace in such a "positive proposition." It is essentially the trace of a desire for some assurance that the future will or can be any better than the present. It is a trace, a residue of the powerful and compulsive desire to be a visionary intellectual, a temptation that lurks in every rhetoric, analytics, politics, and project. The radical critiques of Marxism and Freudianism to be found in Foucault are only the most prominent of his ubiquitous gestures to empty the most characteristic visionary figures of their legitimacy—a legitimacy easily questioned when their associations with not only liberal capitalism and the Gulag but also their quotidian opponents can be traced genealogically.

Deleuze's is certainly the best and most important comment we have yet on Foucault, but it is not exactly the Foucault we need in the current critical context. There is something in Foucault that Deleuze's own project requires that he transform. So that no matter how interesting and important Deleuze's own project, we must be concerned mostly with what he gives us of Foucault and, perhaps even more, with what he puts aside.

What we lose in Deleuze's Foucault is the critically and politically fundamental commitment to enacting the gestures of an ironic negation that would, in itself, exist outside the reach of the reflective apparatus of the State (and its institutions) and its double, the Party. What we lose is both the skeptical questioning of "liberatory" rhetorics and politics and, as important, the anxious pathos that results from having so much to doubt the effects of the great narratives of liberation. What we lose is a certain critical maturity in a time when classical political solutions are impossible; we lose a certain loving despair over the fate of people whose past offers little reason to forget the omnipresence of barbarism as the underside not only of our cultural monuments but of our everyday institutions and rhetorics.

R. P. Blackmur insists that the critic must be "convicted" of knowing the object of his amateurish affection with "internal intimacy."[52] What criticism does can be easily described: "it names and arranges what it knows and loves, and searches endlessly with every fresh impulse or impression for better names and more orderly arrangements." But critics are most inventive in finding ways to flee this task, this "central work of criticism" (p. 373). What critics mostly cannot stand is the discontinuity of knowledge that results from the impossibility of any doctrine expanding to arrange in its own terms all that presents itself.[53] For Blackmur, critics take recourse in heresies—the drive to invent new doctrines when the old ones fail becomes anti-critical just at that moment when the new heresy, for reasons of critical pride and weakness, itself tries to become "omnivorous." Foucault, I think, can perhaps best be caught — fittingly — in the negative of Blackmur's caution:

> For most minds, once doctrine is sighted and is held to be the completion of insight, the doctrinal mode of thinking seems the only one possible. When doctrine totters it seems it can fall only into the gulf of bewilderment; few minds, risk the fall; most seize the remnants and swear the edifice remains, when doctrine becomes intolerable dogma. All fall notwithstanding. . . . [dogmatic] knowledge is dead knowledge; and the worst bewilderment — which is always only comparative — is better than death. . . . We ought scrupulously to risk the use of any concept that seems propitious or helpful in getting over gaps. Only the use should be consciously provisional, speculative, and dramatic. The end-virtue of humility comes only after a long train of humiliations; and the chief labor of humbling is the constant, resourceful restoration of ignorance.[54]

To know how to read the dramatic and tentative use of figures is the lesson of those like Blackmur and Foucault. Yet this use of figures is always in danger of being transformed into a newly marketable model of professional writing and "position taking" or being transmuted, as by Deleuze, into the condition for a new transcendence. Perhaps one must understand Blackmur's own difficult prose and discomfort with the professionalized figure of the writer/critic as part of his marked effort to resist the possible commodification of even the most ironic stance into a critical program. Of course, we might decide that the cost of such quiet and apparent aloofness — no matter how much thoughtful complexity it harbors — is too great a price to pay for preserving criticism over and against all the threats to its ironic integrity. Perhaps such a position abandons too much of the field of overt politics for a dignity of consciousness that too strongly enforces its own pure difference from the messy public world. Yet, one cannot easily answer that the cost is so high that to move toward a position confident of its own goals and assumptions would be the correct thing to do. Jameson correctly says that after reading Foucault one wants an antitranscendent method of reading. But perhaps it should not be a hermeneutic one pursues, not if that means a commitment to one's own developed past imaginings. Rather one should work with a style of reading that is a style of writing — a style that moves at least through Socrates, Montaigne, and Nietzsche to Blackmur and Foucault. One that, perhaps as in Benjamin and Blackmur, rigorously destroys the categories that stabilize the ideologies and institutions of even those we like to think of as "oppositional intellectuals." Perhaps the humility of failure is the only ground for being in opposition since success depends on a very complex knowledge of and ability to manipulate determinative politics, discourses, and institutions — on professional competencies and social privileges that constitute even the "oppositional intellectuals" whose history is so markedly if critically inscribed within the hegemonic in especially postwar practice and theory.[55]

Notes

1. Significantly, a tertiary literature commenting on the proliferation of "Foucault's" has already started up; for a brilliantly satiric example of its pathos see Daniel O'Hara, "What Was Foucault?," in J. Arac, ed. *After Foucault* (New Brunswick: Rutgers University Press, 1988).

2. See Barry Smart, "The Politics of Truth and the Problem of Hegemony," in David Hoy, ed. *Foucault: A Critical Reader* (New York and Oxford: Basil Blackwell, 1986), pp. 157–74.

3. For a particularly sad example of uncritical arrogance that embarrasses everyone involved, see J. G. Merquior, *Foucault* (Berkeley: University of California Press, 1987); originally published by Fontana in 1985 in a series edited by Frank Kermode.

4. See Charles Taylor, "Foucault on Freedom and Truth," in Hoy, *Foucault*, pp. 69–102, hereafter cited as CT in my text.

5. That there is a great difference between the French and North American response to Foucault is, I hope, obvious even if it seems to many Marxist critics that Foucault is a hero to the "neoconservatives," "neoliberals," and "New Philosophers" on both sides of the Atlantic.

6. Of course, I cannot treat all schools of literary criticism as they have variously dealt with Foucault; nor do I mean to suggest they are all the same or all inadequate. For an instance of brilliant critical work powerfully influenced by a careful meditation on Foucault see Jonathan Arac, *Critical Genealogies* (New York: Columbia University Press, 1987). Let me also say that I do not intend to argue that only professional pressures dictate an individual intellectual's response to Foucault. Such a naïve claim could not be defended. I do intend to say that in certain cases, as with analytic Philosophy instanced by

Taylor, the power of professionalized discourse is sufficiently determining for one not to need to explore the other aspects of genealogy
that determine his response to Foucault. The matter for literary criticism, as instanced by the case of Fredric Jameson, as I shall briefly
suggest, is much more complex.

7. Jürgen Habermas, "Modernity versus Postmodernity," trans. Seyla
    Ben-Habib, *NGC*, 22 (Winter 1981), 3–14; Fraser, "Foucault on
    Modern Power," *Praxis International*, 1 (1981), especially pp. 238ff.

8. (Princeton: Princeton University Press, 1979.)

9. Søren Kierkegaard, *Repetition: An Essay in Experimental Psychol-
    ogy*, by Constantine Constantius, trans. Walter Lowrie (New York
    and London: Harper Torchbooks, 1964), p. 33.

10. I should add that I am not here using this term in the complex sense
    given it by Paul de Man, but in a sense far more familiar — at least to
    literary critics — that can be found in such landmark essays as Cleanth
    Brooks's, "The Heresy of Paraphrase," *The Well Wrought Urn* (New
    York: Harcourt, Brace, and World, 1947), pp. 192–214.

11. Michel Foucault, "Truth and Power," *Power/Knowledge*, ed. Colin
    Gordon, trans. Colin Gordon et al. (New York: Pantheon Books,
    1980), p. 131; cited by Taylor in Hoy, p. 93.

12. Michel Foucault, "Two Lectures" (Lecture Two: 14 January 1976),
    Power/Knowledge, p. 93; cited by Taylor in Hoy, p. 94.

13. My disciplinary critique of Taylor converges with Rorty's "imma-
    nent" objections in *Philosophy and the Mirror of Nature*; referring to
    Taylor's work in hermeneutics, Rorty writes: "Taylor reinstates the
    notion of man as a being who changes from the inside by finding bet-
    ter (or, at least, novel) ways of describing, predicting, and explaining
    himself." (Princeton: Princeton University Press, 1979), p. 351.

14. *Power/Knowledge*, p. 93

15. See *Selections from the Prison Notebooks*, ed. and trans. Quintin
    Hoare and Geoffrey Nowell Smith (New York: International Pub-
    lishers, 1971), pp. 6–10.

16. "Her" does not apply here for historical reasons of gender formation.

17. I should perhaps add here that I am concerned with Jameson's work
    in this essay in part precisely because of the way his hostility has had
    the same effect of erasing the help Foucault has been in this project.

18. "Two Lectures," *Power/Knowledge*, p. 130.

19. "Two Lectures," *Power/Knowledge*, p. 131.

20. "Two Lectures," *Power/Knowledge*, p. 131.

21. "Two Lectures," *Power/Knowledge*, p. 131.

22. For an example of the most rigorous thinking on this matter, and of
    the most sensitive reading, one should see an important literary critic,

R. P. Blackmur, "The Critic's Job of Work," *Language as Gesture*
(New York: Columbia University Press, 1981), p. 372; first published
in 1935. One should also see the late Paul de Man's critical meditation
upon the problematic of understanding in *Allegories of Reading* (New
Haven: Yale University Press, 1979).

23. I am aware of the argument that says Taylor has done a service by
taking Foucault seriously before analytic colleagues for whom Foucault, like his great predecessors Nietzsche, Marx, and Freud, is no
"philosopher." I reject this because there are different tactical effects
in this "taking seriously," and I am not certain that making Foucault
seem worthwhile to Anglo-American Professors of analytic Philosophy is not, in itself, too costly a compromise. Of course, I am contend-
ing fundamentally that Taylor renders Foucault "senseless" rather
than "serious."

24. Cf. *Power/Knowledge*, p. 119ff.

25. Cf. Paul A. Bové, *Intellectuals in Power* (New York: Columbia
University Press, 1986).

26. See Merquior, note 3 above.

27. When I say "dominant," I am not unaware of the pluralist line in the
humanities that insists there are varieties of people and methods with
real differences among them. I am the last to deny those differences
wherever they can be found. But that these pluralist claims usually
mask a practice and "ideology" of "dedifferentiation" akin to what
Donald Pease calls "consensus formation" in his *Visionary Compact*
(Madison: University of Wisconsin Press, 1986) can be seen by reex-
amining Northrop Frye's *Anatomy of Literature* (Princeton: Princeton University Press, 1957).

28. This is a point often made by Edward W. Said apropos his reading
of both Foucault and Gramsci. See *Orientalism* (New York: Pantheon
Books, 1978), and, for example, p. 39ff.

29. By futural I mean what the Black Mountain Poets, following on
Whitman, would have called the "projective," or what Nietzsche
would call the prophetic and life-giving. Cf. Paul A. Bové, *Destructive Poetics* (New York: Columbia University Press, 1980), pp.
131–81; 217–81.

30. In his talk on Foucault and Central European politics presented at
SUNY/Binghamton on December 2, 1987, Jonathan Arac developed
this point in his comment on Michael Walzer's reading of Foucault
in Hoy, *Foucault: A Critical Reader*, pp. 51–68.

31. *In the Tracks of Historical Materialism* (London: Verso Editions,
1983), p. 49.

32. *In the Tracks of Historical Materialism*, p. 50.

33. Edward W. Said, *Orientalism* (New York: Pantheon Books, 1978), p. 25; the original passage in Gramsci can be found in *Quaderni del Carcere*, ed. Valentino Gerratana (Turin: Einaudi Editore, 1975) 2: 1363.
34. (Ithaca: Cornell University Press, 1981), pp. 21ff.
35. Trans. Robert Hurley et al. (New York: Viking, 1977).
36. That he does do so later is clear from pp. 90–91.
37. (Princeton: Princeton University Press, 1971), especially pp. 110ff.
38. *The Political Unconscious*, p. 90.
39. Of course, if one chooses, one can hear in this not only a critique of certain dominant moments in the West, but of the command or planned economies of the (pre-Gorbachevian?) of "actually existing socialism."
40. For example, Jameson could give a more textured analysis of this "dualism" within his own terms: the opposition between Freedom and Necessity submerged within the forgotten narrative of human struggle surely allows for a more "realistic" analysis of the specific historical struggles taking place in the texts he labels "total systems." In other words, he needs simply to follow Sartre's use of the "project" in his analysis of the Gironde as Jameson himself studies it in *Marxism and Form*. Perhaps, however, the problem lies at a deeper level, one suggested by Lukács's influence (rather than Sartre's) over Jameson, especially that Lukács who so highly values realism because it reproduces character "types" and by contrast with which Modernist critical investigations into the specificity of texts and figures can be dismissed as "the 'conversion' of the critic" to the Modernists' demands for critical assent to the "optical illusion of totality projected by what is in reality only an artificial isolation." (See *Marxism and Form*, p. 315.) Jameson's career can be understood, in one sense, as the attempt to differentiate orthodoxy from heterodoxy and heresy in the matter of the "totality."
41. It is worth pointing out that there are at least two uses of "unmasking" in *The Political Unconscious*; one that marks the legitimate task of Marxist intellectuals in their practice of tracing the presence of the political unconscious and a second that is a form of neoconservative intellectual practice of the sort that would allow such an intellectual to "unmask" an apparently hidden complicity of the oppositional with the dominant and, in so doing, apparently dismiss the oppositional once and for all.
42. See *Marxism and Form*, pp. 230–32. It can do this by doing away with the false sense, essential to each successive "project," that each

is an effort to totalize, and so do away with the need for theorizing a life or career as a succession of abandoned and reformed "projects."
43. See Bové, *Intellectuals in Power*, especially Chapter 5.
44. See R. P. Blackmur, "Language as Gesture," in *Language as Gesture*, pp. 3–24.
45. Jean Baudrillard, *Oublier Foucault* (Paris: Editions Galilé, 1977).
46. *The Political Unconscious*, p. 91.
47. Trans. Hugh Tomlinson. (New York: Columbia University Press, 1983.) Originally published in French as *Nietzsche et la philosophie*. (Paris: Presses Universitaires de France, 1962.)
48. This is a problem that has concerned me elsewhere, especially Chapter 6 of *Intellectuals in Power*.
49. See especially Julian Roberts, *Walter Benjamin* (Atlantic Highlands, NJ: Humanities Press, 1983), pp. 7ff.
50. See Cornel West, *The American Evasion of Philosophy: A Genealogy of Pragmatism* (Madison: University of Wisconsin Press, 1989); and Barry Smart's very important essay "The Politics of Truth and the Problem of Hegemony," in Hoy, pp. 157–73.
51. See Bové, *Intellectuals in Power* for a fuller discussion of Foucault's commitment to critical negation.
52. "The Critic's Job of Work," *Language as Gesture*, p. 372.
53. One might do well to remember that Jameson values Marxism's central figure of the "mode of production" just because it offers the possibility of imagining such expansion. Of course, this marks Jameson's form of opposition as inscribed within critical reflection and suggests its origins in Gramsci's adaptation of a World War I metaphor, namely "the war of position." Cf. *The Political Unconscious*, p. 21.
54. "The Critic's Job of Work," pp. 373–74.
55. See Bové, *Intellectuals in Power*, passim.

Translating Theory, or the Difference between Deleuze and Foucault

'Perhaps one day this century will be known as Deleuzian.'[1]
Foucault's claim at the beginning of his essay 'Theatrum
Philosophicum' contrasts sharply with Foucault's own much
greater reputation in the English-speaking world. Various
reasons have been given as to why today there are still no
'Deleuzians'.[2] Deleuze's post-Kantianism does not offer the
comfort of a continually rehearsed orthodoxy; instead, even
his more conventional philosophical histories force a constant
re-evaluation of the standard panoply of Western thought.[3]
These impeccable readings do not provide a rush of blood to
the head, or students to the seminar. This is in turn com-
plicated by the wide range of his work: his history of
philosophy is supplemented by the critical philosophy of
Différence et répétition and *Logique du sens* (1969), the extraordinary collaboration with Félix Guattari which has produced the *Anti-Oedipus* (1972) and the *Thousand Plateaus*
(1980), and the aesthetic works on Proust (1964), Francis
Bacon (1981) and cinema (1983 and 1985).

But this in itself is not of great importance. Indeed, it even
provides the opportunity for us to follow up Foucault's remark
in a way that makes redundant the search for a Master. As
Foucault puts it: 'thought is again possible' (*TP*, p. 196). For
both Deleuze and Foucault recognize that the relationship
between their work resembles the partial and fragmentary
relationships between theory and practice that can no longer

be understood in terms of totalization. This claim is made most specifically in two places. The first is in a recorded discussion, 'Intellectuals and Power'.[4] Here, in a wide-ranging conversation that takes in Marxism, the Group for Information about Prisons founded by Foucault, the evolution of politics in modern France, Vietnam and May '68, both thinkers constantly reiterate that 'theory does not express, translate, or serve to apply practice: it is practice' (*IP*, p. 208). It is therefore not a totalizing instrument, but one that multiplies potentialities. It is in this sense that Foucault wishes to call the century 'Deleuzian', or Deleuze sees 'Foucault' as one of those great works that have changed our conception of thinking (p. 128). The second place in which this is affirmed is in Foucault's preface to the English edition of the *Anti-Oedipus*.[5] Here Foucault specifically regards the work of Deleuze and Guattari as being an ethics, or an 'Introduction to the Non-Fascist Life', that contains essential de-individualizing principles:

Free political action from all unitary and totalizing paranoia.

Develop action, thought, and desires by proliferation, juxtaposition, and disjunction, and not by subdivision and pyramidal hierarchization.

Withdraw allegiance from the old categories of the Negative (law limit, castration, lack, lacuna), which Western thought has so long held sacred as a form of power and an access to reality. Prefer what is positive and multiple: difference over uniformity, flows over unities, mobile arrangements over systems. Believe that what is productive is not sedentary but nomadic.

Do not think that one has to be sad in order to be militant, even though the thing one is fighting is abominable. It is the connection of desire to reality (and not its retreat into the forms of representation) that possesses revolutionary force.

Do not use thought to ground a political practice in

Truth; nor political action to discredit, as mere speculation, a line of thought. Use political practice as an intensifier of thought, and analysis as a multiplier of the forms and domains for the intervention of political action.

Do not demand of politics that it restore the 'rights' of the individual, as philosophy has defined them. The individual is the product of power. What is needed is to 'de-individualize' by means of multiplication and displacement, diverse combinations. The group must not be the organic bond uniting hierarchized individuals, but a constant generator of de-individualization.

Do not become enamoured of power.

If the century will be known as 'Deleuzian', therefore, it will be because of the decentrings which such an ethics brings about. In 'Theatrum Philosophicum' Foucault is interested in Deleuze's 'reversed Platonism' which does not turn the relationship between them as philosophers into an architecture of systems, but discloses instead the division already existing within any philosophy of essences. The inaccessible Idea will be displaced by the smallest detail. This articulates a 'philosophy of the phantasm' behind which there does not lurk the real truth. The phantasm exists on the level of the body, as well as outside the body to the extent that it exists between bodies: it topologizes the body's materiality. This polyscenic theatre, 'the gesturing of hands and fingers' (*TP*, p. 171), provides us with a metaphysics, or 'phantasmaphysics', that overturns the philosophy of representation. The obverse of Platonism is therefore a philosophy of the pure event. An event is not a state that may serve as a referent, but it leads instead to a new form of philosophy, one that gives us 'a metaphysics of the incorporeal event [. . .] a logic of neutral meaning [. . .] and a thought of the present infinitive' (*TP*, p. 176). If we determine an event on the basis of a concept, we fall into Knowing; if we measure the phantasm against its supposed origin in reality, we are judging. These two conditions, the concept and the philosophy of representation, make up 'Philosophy'; whereas *thinking* as an event is a repetition without a model, a dice-throw. This nomadic, rather than sedentary, thinking produces difference within its very repetitions.[6]

Once thought is no longer devoted to the building of concepts in this way, difference is seen as a pure event. Thought can then be perceived as 'the vertical dimension of intensities, because intensity, well before its gradation by representation, is in itself pure difference' (*TP*, p. 183). This liberation of pure difference leads to the abandonment of dialectics and a move to an affirmative thought of disjunction and multiplicity. A fourth condition for thinking of the phantasm and the event thus arises: the abandonment of categories and the move to an acategorical thought.

This Leirisian fibrillation of Becoming, so clearly perceived in Deleuze by Foucault, is the very principle of Deleuze's history of philosophy. Here he entertains a series of *relations*. In Empiricism, the Stoics, Spinoza and Nietzsche, a strict complementarity is established between physical states and metaphysical events, such that thought or entity is an event and never a concept. Deleuze's reading of Foucault follows the same pattern, one that escapes the system of Law-and-Sovereign. Indeed, their relation of mutual immanence is above all philosophy's relation to itself, a repetition that reveals the maximum difference within identity: a non-identity. This folding produces a philosophy that is not a concept but an event, an ontology of the present that works against the dialectic.

Deleuze gives this thought of the phantasm and the event the proper name of 'Foucault'. It might also properly be called translation: a disjunctive affirmation, the emergence of a new form.

Seán Hand

Acknowledgements

To regain pure language fully formed in the linguistic flux,
is the tremendous and only capacity of translation. In this
pure language — which no longer means or expresses anything but is, as expressionless and creative Word, that
which is meant in all languages — all information, all sense,
and all intention finally encounter a stratum in which they
are destined to be extinguished
  (W. Benjamin, 'The Task of the Translator', in
Illuminations [London: Fontana, 1982], p. 80).

I should like to thank several people who have helped me
through the stratum of translation. Gilles Deleuze offered
clear advice and encouragement. Jonathan Rée gave me the
opportunity to discuss my work in a warm and stimulating
environment. Jean-Jacques Lecercle provided genuine
friendship. Ursula Goggs of Athlone nurtured the project with
efficiency and enthusiasm. Staff at the Bodleian Library, and
the Taylorian Library, Oxford were most helpful. Students
and colleagues at the University College of Wales,
Aberystwyth, braved endless questions about the meaning
and translatability of terms. Margaret Parry displayed
extraordinary stamina and serenity in typing the whole
manuscript. Above all, Maolíosa continues to endure my vain
search for 'the immortal word'. As ever, I dedicate this task to
her.

Abbreviations

AK   *The Archaeology of Knowledge*, trans. A. Sheridan
     (London: Tavistock and New York: Pantheon, 1972).

AS   *L'archéologie du savoir* (Paris: Gallimard, 1969).

BC   *The Birth of the Clinic*, trans. A. Sheridan (London:
     Tavistock and New York: Pantheon, 1973).

CNP *Ceci n'est pas une pipe* (Montpellier: Fata Morgana,
     1973).

DL   *Death and the Labyrinth: the World of Raymond Roussel*,
     trans. C. Ruas (New York: Doubleday, 1986 and
     London: Athlone, 1987).

DP   *Discipline and Punish. Birth of the Prison*, trans. A.
     Sheridan (London: Allen Lane and New York:
     Pantheon, 1977; reprinted Harmondsworth: Peregrine,
     1979).

HF   *Histoire de la folie à l'âge classique* (Paris: Gallimard,
     1972).

HS   *The History of Sexuality, vol. 1: An Introduction*, trans. R.
     Hurley (New York: Pantheon, 1978 and Harmonds-
     worth: Penguin, 1984).

IPR *I, Pierre Rivière* . . . trans. F. Jellinek (New York:
     Pantheon, 1975 and Harmondsworth: Peregrine, 1978).

LCP *Language, Counter-Memory, Practice*, edited by D.
     Bouchard (Oxford: Blackwell, 1977).

LIM 'The life of infamous men', in *Power, Truth, Strategy*,
     edited by M. Morris and P. Patton (Sydney: Feral
     Publications, 1979) pp. 76–91.

MAC *Madness and Civilization*, trans. R. Howard (New York:

Random House, 1965 and London: Tavistock, 1967).

MC *Les mots et les choses* (Paris: Gallimard, 1966).

MPR *Moi, Pierre Rivière.* . . (Paris: Gallimard-Julliard, ouvrage collectif, 1973).

NC *Naissance de la clinique* (Paris: Presses Universitaires de France, 1963; revised 1972).

NGH 'Nietzsche, la généalogie, l'histoire', in *Hommage à Jean Hyppolite* (Paris: Presses Universitaires de France, 1971). 'Nietzsche, Genealogy, History', trans. D. Bouchard and S. Simon, in *LCP*, pp. 139–64.

OD *L'ordre du discours* (Paris: Gallimard, 1971).

OT *The Order of Things*, trans. A. Sheridan (London: Tavistock and New York: Pantheon, 1970).

PDD 'La pensée du dehors', *Critique*, No. 229 (June 1966): 523–46.

QA *'Qu'est-ce qu'un auteur?'*, *Bulletin de la Société française de philosophie*, 63, No. 3 (1969), 73–104.

RR *Raymond Roussel* (Paris: Gallimard, 1963).

SP *Surveiller et punir. Naissance de la prison* (Paris: Gallimard, 1975).

SS *Le souci de soi* (Histoire de la sexualité III) (Paris: Gallimard, 1984).

TDL *'The Discourse on Language', trans. R. Swyer, in The Archaeology of Knowledge* (New York, 1972).

TNP *This is not a pipe*, trans. James Harkness (Berkeley: University of California Press, 1981).

TUP *The Use of Pleasure*, trans. R. Hurley (New York: Random House, 1985 and Harmondsworth: Viking, 1986).

UP *L'usage des plaisirs* (Histoire de la sexualité II) (Paris: Gallimard, 1984).

VHI 'La vie des hommes infâmes', *Les cahiers du chemin* 29 (1977), pp. 12–29.

VS *La volonté de savoir* (Histoire de la sexualité I) (Paris: Gallimard, 1976).

WA 'What is an Author', trans. D. Bouchard and S. Simon, in *LCP*, pp. 113–38.

FROM THE ARCHIVE TO THE DIAGRAM

A New Archivist

(The Archaeology of Knowledge)

A new archivist has been appointed. But has anyone actually appointed him? Is he not rather acting on his own instructions? Certain malevolent people say that he is the new representative of a structural technology or technocracy. Others, mistaking their insults for wit, claim that he is a supporter of Hitler, or at least that he offends the rights of man (they will not forgive him for having proclaimed the 'death of man').[1] Some say that he is a shammer who cannot back himself up with reference to the sacred texts, and who seldom quotes the great philosophers. Others, though, claim that something radically new has appeared in philosophy, and that this work is as beautiful as those it challenges. It celebrates the dawn of a new age.

In any case, it all begins like a story by Gogol[1] (rather than by Kafka). The new archivist proclaims that henceforth he will deal only with statements. He will not concern himself with what previous archivists have treated in a thousand different ways: propositions and phrases. He will ignore both the vertical hierarchy of propositions which are stacked on top of one another, and the horizontal relationship established between phrases in which each seems to respond to another. Instead he will remain mobile, skimming along in a kind of diagonal line that allows him to read what could not be apprehended before, namely statements. Is this perhaps an atonal logic? It is natural for us to have misgivings. For the

archivist deliberately refuses to give examples. He believes
that he never stopped giving them in the past, even if at the
time he was unaware that they were examples. Now the only
formal example he analyses is intended to be disquieting: a
series of letters which I might write down at random, or
record in the order in which they appear on the keyboard of a
typewriter: 'The keyboard of a typewriter is not a statement;
but the same series of letters, A, Z, E, R, T, listed in a
typewriting manual, is the statement of the alphabetical order
adopted by French typewriters.'[2] Such multiplicities have no
set linguistic construction, yet they are statements. Azert?
Since we are used to the approach of other archivists, we find
ourselves wondering how Foucault can possibly produce
statements under these conditions.

This is especially true since Foucault asserts that
statements are essentially *rare*. This is the case *de facto* and *de
jure*: they are necessarily tied to a law and an effect of rarity.
Indeed, this is one of the characteristics that make them
different from propositions and phrases. For propositions can
be thought of in any number of ways, since we can use the
differences between types to express any one in terms of the
others. Such a formalization does not have to distinguish
between what is possible and what is real; it generates possible
propositions. As for what is really said, its *de facto* rarity comes
about because one phrase denies the existence of others, for-
bidding, contradicting or repressing them to such an extent
that each phrase remains pregnant with everything left unsaid. This virtual or latent content multiplies meaning and
opens itself up to interpretation, creating a 'hidden discourse'
that *de jure* is a source of great richness. A dialectic of phrases
is always open to contradiction, even if the end result merely
overcomes or reinforces that contradiction; while a typology of
propositions lays itself open to abstraction, and so creates a
type for each level that is in fact superior to its constituent
elements. But contradiction and abstraction are the means by
which phrases and propositions are multiplied, since one

phrase can always be opposed to another, or one proposition formed on the basis of another.

Statements, on the other hand, inhabit a general realm of rarity within which they are distributed begrudgingly and even inadequately. No sense of possibility or potentiality exists in the realm of statements. Everything in them is real and all reality is manifestly present. All that counts is what has been formulated at a given moment, including any blanks and gaps. It is none the less certain that statements can be opposed to one another, and placed in hierarchical order. But in the space of two chapters Foucault rigorously demonstrates that contradictions between statements can be measured only by calculating the concrete distance between them within this space of rarity. Comparisons between statements are therefore linked to a mobile diagonal line that allows us, within this space, to make a direct study of the same set at different levels, as well as to choose some sets on the same level while disregarding others (which in their turn might presuppose another diagonal line).[3] It is precisely the rarefied nature of this space which creates these unusual movements and bursts of passion that cut space up into new dimensions. To our amazement, this 'incomplete, fragmented form' shows, when it comes to statements, how not only few things are said, but 'few things can be said'.[4] What consequences from this transportation of logic will find their way into that element of rarity or dispersion which has nothing to do with negativity, but which on the contrary forms that 'positivity' which is unique to statements?

Foucault also tries to reassure us, though: if it is true that statements are essentially rare, no originality is needed in order to produce them. A statement always represents a transmission of particular elements distributed in a corresponding space. As we shall see, the formations and transformations of these spaces themselves pose topological problems that cannot adequately be described in terms of creation, beginning or foundation. When studying a particular space, it matters even less whether a statement has taken place for the first time, or whether it involves repetition or reproduction. What counts is the *regularity* of the statement: it represents not the average, but rather the whole statistical curve. In effect the statement is to be associated not with the transmission of particular elements presupposed by it but with the shape of the whole curve to which they are related, and more generally with the rules governing the particular field in which they are distributed and reproduced. This is what characterizes the regularity of statements:

> The originality/banality opposition is therefore not relevant: between an initial formulation and the sentence, which, years, centuries later, repeats it more or less exactly, [the archaeological description] establishes no hierarchy of value; it makes no radical difference. It tries only to establish the *regularity* of statements.[5]

The question of originality is all the more rare for the fact that the question of origins is never raised at all. It is not necessary to be someone to produce a statement, and the statement does not refer back to any *Cogito* or transcendal subject that might render it possible, or to any ego that might pronounce it for the first time (or recommence it), or to any Spirit of the Age that could conserve, propagate and recuperate it.[6] There are many places from which any subject can produce the same statement, and they vary greatly. But precisely because different individuals can intervene in each case, a statement accumulates into a specific object which then becomes preserved, transmitted or repeated. This accumulation resembles the building up of a stock of provisions; it is not the opposite of rarity, but an effect of this same rarity. In this way it replaces notions of origin and return to origins: like Bergsonian memory, a statement preserves itself within its own space and continues to exist while this space endures or is reconstituted.

We must distinguish between three different realms of space which encircle any statement. First of all there is *collateral space*, an associate or adjacent domain formed from other statements that are part of the same group. The question of knowing whether the space defines the group or, conversely, whether the group of statements defines the space, is immaterial. There is no homogeneous space that remains unlocalized: the two elements merge at the level of the rules of formation. The important point is that these rules of formation cannot be reduced either to axioms, as in the case of propositions, or to a single context, as in the case of phrases. Propositions refer vertically to axioms on a higher level which in turn determine certain constant and intrinsic factors and define a homogeneous system. The establishment of such homogeneous systems is indeed one of the conditions of linguistics. As for phrases, one of their members can be found in one system and another in a different system, in accordance with certain extrinsic variable factors.

A statement, however, is something completely different: it is inseparable from an inherent variant. Consequently, we never remain wholly within a single system but are continually passing from one to the other (even within a single language). A statement operates neither laterally nor vertically but transversally, and its rules are to be found on the same level as itself. Perhaps Foucault and Labov are similar in this respect, especially when the latter demonstrates how a young Black can move back and forth between 'black English' and 'standard American' in accordance with rules which are in themselves *variable* or *optional* and which allow us to define regularities but not homogeneities.[7] Even when they seem to operate within the same language, statements of a discursive formation move from description to observation, calculation, institution and prescription, and use several systems or languages in the process.[8] A group or family of statements is in fact 'formed' by rules of change or variation to be found on the same level, and these rules make the 'family' a medium for dispersion and heterogeneity, the very opposite of a homogeneity.

This is the nature of the associate or adjacent space: each statement is inseparable via certain rules of change (vectors). And not only is each statement in this way inseparable from a multiplicity that is both 'rare' and regular, but each statement is itself a multiplicity, not a structure or a system. This topology of statements contrasts both with the typology of propositions and with the dialectic of phrases. It is our belief that a statement, a family of statements, or a discursive formation is first of all defined for Foucault by certain inherent lines of variation or by a field of vectors which cut through the associate space: the statement therefore exists as a *primitive function*, or as the first meaning of the term 'regularity'.

The second area is that of *correlative space*, which is not to be confused with the associate space. Here we are concerned with the link which a statement entertains, not with other statements but with its subjects, objects and concepts. In this we might discover new differences between a statement on the one hand and words, phrases or propositions on the other. In fact phrases are linked to a so-called subject of enunciation who seemingly has the power to begin a discourse: this involves a linguistic 'I' that cannot be reduced to 'he' even when it is not explicitly formulated, since it sets things in motion or is self-referential. The phrase is therefore analysed from the double viewpoint of the intrinsic constant (the form of the 'I') and the extrinsic variables (where he who says 'I' creates a sense of form). The situation is completely different for a statement, which refers back not to a unique form but to certain intrinsic positions which are extremely variable and form part of the statement itself. For example, if a 'literary' statement refers us back to an author, an anonymous letter can equally imply an author, but in a completely different sense; while an ordinary letter refers to a signatory, a contract necessitates an underwriter, a poster implies a copywriter, a collection indicates the existence of a compiler, and so on.[9] All this forms part of a statement, even though it has nothing to do with the nature of a phrase: it is a function *derived* from the primitive function: that is, a function derived from the statement.

The link between the statement and a variable subject in itself constitutes a variable that is intrinsic to the statement. In 'For a long time I used to go to bed early . . .' the phrase remains the same, while the statement appears different according to whether or not we associate it with a specific subject or with the author Proust, who uses it to begin *A la Recherche du temps perdu* and attributes it to a narrator. The same statement can therefore offer several different positions for the speaking subject, involving an author and a narrator or a signatory and an author, as in a letter by Mme de Sévigné (since the addressee is not the same in each case), or a reporter and whatever is reported, as in indirect speech (and above all in free indirect speech, where the two different positions occupied by the speaking subject imply one another).

But all these positions are not the various forms of a primordial 'I' from which a statement stems: on the contrary, these positions stem from the statement itself and consequently become the categories of 'non-person', 'he', 'one', 'He speaks' or 'One speaks', which are defined by the family of statements. Here Foucault echoes Blanchot in denouncing all linguistic personology and seeing the different positions for the speaking subject as located within a deep anonymous murmur. It is within this murmur without beginning or end that Foucault would like to be situated, in the place assigned to him by statements.[10] And perhaps these are Foucault's most moving statements.

We can say as much for the objects and concepts of a statement. A proposition is supposed to have a referent. That is to say that while reference or intentionality is intrinsic and constant in propositions, whatever fulfils that purpose is extrinsic and variable. But this is not the case with statements: a statement has a 'discursive object' which does not derive in any sense from a particular state of things, but stems from the statement itself. It is a derived object, defined precisely by the limits to the lines of variation of the statement existing as a primitive function. As a result there is no point in distinguishing between the different types of intentionality; some could be furnished by the condition of things, while others would remain empty and offer instead an example of generally fictive or imaginary states (I met a unicorn) or even generally absurd ones (a squared circle).

Sartre said that each dream and dream-image differed from a continual state of hypnosis or the ordinary state of being awake in that it inhabited its own special world.[11] Foucault's statements are like these dreams: each one has its own special object or world. So 'The golden mountain is in California' is indeed a statement: it has no referent, but one cannot simply invoke an empty intentionality where anything goes (fiction in general). The statement 'The golden mountain . . .' does have a discursive object, namely the specific imaginary world that 'does or does not authorize such a geological or geographical fantasy' (we can understand this more easily if we consider the statement 'A diamond as big as the Ritz', which does not relate back to fiction in general but rather to that very specific world which surrounds any statement by Scott Fitzgerald. This statement therefore links up with other statements by the same author, and together they make up a 'family').[12]

The same conclusion holds for concepts: a concept stands as a word's signified, that is to say as an extrinsic variable, to which it is related by virtue of its signifiers (an intrinsic constant). But here again the same does not hold for statements. The latter possess their own discursive concepts or 'schemata': these are to be found at the intersection of different systems and are cut across by the statement acting in the role of primitive function. This can be seen in the groupings and contrasts which medical statements make between various different symptoms at any particular age of discursive formation (which accounts for the general transformation of seventeenth-century mania into nineteenth-century monomania).[13]

If statements can be distinguished from words, phrases or propositions, it is because they contain their own functions of subject, object and concept in the form of 'derivatives'. To be precise, subject, object and concept are merely functions derived from the primitive function or from the statement. As a result, the correlative space is the discursive order of places or positions occupied by subjects, objects and concepts in a family of statements. This is the second sense of 'regularity', for these different places represent particular points. The system of words, phrases and propositions, which operates through the use of an intrinsic contrast and an extrinsic variable, differs fundamentally from the multiplicity of statements, which operates on the principle of an inherent variation and an intrinsic variable. What seems accidental from the viewpoint of words, phrases and propositions becomes the rule from the viewpoint of statements. In this way Foucault lays the foundations for a new pragmatics.

This still leaves the third, extrinsic, realm of space: the *complementary space* of non-discursive formations ('instructions, political events, economic practices and processes'). It is here that Foucault begins to outline his conception of a political philosophy. Any institution implies the existence of statements such as a constitution, a charter, contracts, registrations and enrolments. Conversely, statements refer back to an institutional milieu which is necessary for the formation both of the objects which arise in such examples of the statement and of the subject who speaks from this position (for example the position of the writer in society, the position of the doctor in the hospital or at his surgery, in any given period, together with the new emergence of objects). But here again, between the non-discursive formations of institutions and the discursive formations of statements, there is a great temptation to establish either a sort of vertical parallelism such as might exist between two expressions symbolizing one another (primary relations of expression) or a horizontal causality in which events and institutions would determine

the nature of the supposed author of the statement (secondary
relations of reflection). At all events, a diagonal movement
creates a third possibility: discursive relations become
associated with non-discursive milieux, which are not in
themselves situated either inside or outside the group of
statements but form the above-mentioned limit, the specific
horizon without which these objects could neither appear nor
be assigned a place in the statement itself:

> Not, of course, that it was political practice that from the
> early nineteenth century imposed on medicine such new
> objects as tissular lesions or the anatomo-physiological
> correlations; but it opened up new fields for the mapping of
> medical objects ([. . .] the mass of the population
> administratively compartmented and supervised [. . .] the
> great conscript armies [. . .] the institutions of hospital
> assistance that were defined at the end of the eighteenth
> and the beginning of the nineteenth centuries, in relation to
> the economic needs of the time and to the reciprocal posi-
> tion of the social classes). One can also see the appearance
> of this relation of political practice to medical discourse in
> the status accorded to the doctor [. . .].[14]

Since the distinction between originality and banality is no
longer pertinent, a statement may be repeated. A phrase may
be begun again or re-evoked, a proposition may be
reactualized, but only 'the statement may be *repeated*'.[15] None
the less, it appears that the real conditions under which repetition may take place are very strict. The area of distribution, the allocation of unique elements, the sequence of
place and event, the link established with an instituted milieu
– in each case all these must be the same in order to give the
statement a 'materiality' that makes it repeatable. 'Species
evolve' is not the same statement when used first by
eighteenth-century history and then by nineteenth-century
biology. It is not certain that the statement remains the same
even from Darwin to Simpson, given that the description in

each case might raise completely different units of measure, distances, distributions and even institutions. The same slogan: 'Put madmen in the asylum!' can belong to discursive formations that are completely distinct from one another, depending on whether it is an eighteenth-century protest against confusing prisoners with madmen or a nineteenth-century demand for asylums in order to separate madmen from prisoners, or even a present-day objection to change within the hospital service.[16]

We might object that all Foucault is doing is refining a very classical analysis that relies on *context*. This would ignore the novelty of the criteria which he institutes, precisely in order to show that one can articulate a phrase or formulate a proposition without always occupying the same place in the corresponding statement, and without reproducing the same particular features. And if one is led to denounce false repetitions by determining the discursive formation to which a statement belongs, one equally uncovers certain isomorphisms or isotopisms lurking between distinct formations.[17] Context explains nothing, since its nature varies according to the particular discursive formation or family of statements under consideration.[18]

If the repetition of statements is subject to such strict conditions, this is not by virtue of external conditions but as a result of that internal materiality that makes repetition itself the power that a statement is alone in possessing. A statement always defines itself by establishing a specific link with *something else* that lies on the same level as itself: that is, something else which concerns the statement itself (and not the meaning or elements of that statement). This 'other thing' may also be a statement, in which case the statement openly repeats itself. But rather than being a statement, almost inevitably it is something foreign, something outside. That is to say, it involves the pure transmission of unique elements which remain indeterminate points, since they are not yet defined and limited by the curve of the statement that joins them up and assumes a certain form in their presence. Foucault shows, then, that a curve, a graph, a pyramid are statements, but that what they represent is not a statement. Similarly the letters written out by me, AZERT, are a statement, even though these same letters do not form a statement on the keyboard.[19]

In this case we observe how a secret repetition animates the statement, and the reader is once more faced with the theme of 'the tiny difference that paradoxically creates identity' which inspired the best pages of *Raymond Roussel*. A statement is in itself a repetition, even if what it repeats is 'something else' that none the less 'is strangely similar and almost identical to it'. So the greatest problem for Foucault would be to uncover the nature of these peculiar features presupposed by the statement. But *The Archaeology of Knowledge* stops at this point and does not attempt to deal with a problem that surpasses the limits of 'knowledge'. Foucault's readers become aware of the fact that we are entering into a new domain, that of power and its relation to knowledge, which is to be explained by the sequel to *Archaeology*. But already we feel that AZERT, on the keyboard, represents the focal point of power or of power-relations between the letters of the French alphabet, depending on which one crops up, and the typist's fingers, depending on which one is used.

As Foucault explains, *The Order of Things* deals neither with things nor with words. It is not concerned with object or subject, nor does it examine phrases or propositions, grammatical analysis, logic or semantics. Statements are not in any sense portrayed as a synthesis of words and things, or as composite phrases or propositions. On the contrary, they precede the phrases or propositions which implicitly presuppose them, and lead to the formation of words and objects. There are two moments when Foucault goes back on this: in *Madness and Civilization* he has recourse too often to an 'experience' of madness that is already inscribed in a duality existing between the states of raw things and propositions;

and in *The Birth of the Clinic* he invokes a 'medical gaze' that still relies on a unitary subject whose position never changes with regard to objects.

All the same, these lapses are perhaps fake. It is no cause for regret that the romanticism which contributed to the beauty of *Madness and Civilization* has been abandoned in favour of a new positivism. This rarefied form of positivism, which in itself is poetic, perhaps helps to rekindle a general experience in the dissemination of discursive formations or statements, an experience which is still that of madness; while it also reintroduces into the various locations at the heart of these formations a mobile site which is still that of a doctor, clinician, diagnostician or symptomatologist of civilizations (independently of any *Weltanschauung*). And what is the conclusion to *Archaeology* if not an appeal to a general theory of production which must merge with revolutionary praxis, and where the acting 'discourse' is formed within an 'outside' that remains indifferent to my life and death? For discursive formations are real practices, and far from being a universal logos their languages are transient and tend to promote and sometimes even to express mutation.

So this is our definition of a group of statements, or even a single statement: they are multiplicities. It was Riemann in the field of physics and mathematics who dreamed up the notion of 'multiplicity' and different kinds of multiplicities. The philosophical importance of this notion then appeared in Husserl's *Formal and Transcendental Logic*, and in Bergson's *Essay on the Immediate Given of Awareness* (where he tries to define duration as a type of multiplicity to be contrasted with spatial multiplicities, rather as Riemann had distinguished between discrete and continuous multiplicities). But the notion died out in these two areas, either because it became obscured by a newly restored simple dualism arising from a distinction made between genres, or because it tended to assume the status of an axiomatic system.

None the less, the core of the notion is the constitution of a substantive in which 'multiple' ceases to be a predicate opposed to the One, or attributable to a subject identified as one. Multiplicity remains completely indifferent to the traditional problems of the multiple and the one, and above all to the problem of a subject who would think through this multiplicity, give it conditions, account for its origins, and so on. There is neither one nor multiple, which would at all events entail having recourse to a consciousness that would be regulated by the one and developed by the other. There are only rare multiplicities composed of particular elements, empty places for those who temporarily function as subjects, and cumulable, repeatable and self-preserving regularities. Multiplicity is neither axiomatic nor typological, but topological. Foucault's book represents the most decisive step yet taken in the theory-practice of multiplicities.

In another sense this is also the path taken by Maurice Blanchot's logic of literary production, which maintains the most rigorous link between the singular and the plural, the neutral and repetition, in such a way as to challenge simultaneously the form given to consciousness or a subject and the bottomlessness of an undifferentiated abyss. Foucault has not disguised the way in which he feels akin to Blanchot. And he demonstrates how the heart of contemporary debates has less to do with structuralism as such – that is, with the existence (or lack of it) of models and realities that we call structures – than with the place and status bestowed on the subject in ways we feel are not completely structured. Therefore, as long as we continue to contrast history directly with structure, we persist in believing that the subject can gather, build up and unify matter. But this no longer holds true if we think of 'epochs' or historical formations as being multiplicities. The latter escape from both the reign of the subject and the empire of struture. Structure is propositional, has an axiomatic nature that can be tied to a specific level and forms a homogeneous system, while a statement is a multiplicity that passes through all levels and 'cuts across a domain of structures and possible unities, and which reveals them, with concrete contents, in time and space.'[20] The subject is the product of phrases or dialectic and has the character of a first person with whom discourse begins, while the statement is an anonymous function which leaves a trace of subject only in the third person, as a derived function.

Archaeology contrasts with the two principal techniques used until now by 'archivists': formalization and interpretation. Archivists have often jumped from one technique to the other, while relying on both at the same time. Sometimes their analysis of a phrase isolates a logical proposition which then operates as its manifest meaning: in this way they move beyond what is 'inscribed' to an intelligent form, which no doubt in turn can be inscribed on a symbolic surface but is in itself of a different order to that of the inscription. On other occasions, however, they move from one plane to a second, and see the two as being secretly related: in this way the initial inscription is doubled by a second inscription. The latter no doubt contains a hidden meaning but, above all, it is not the same in terms either of inscription or of content.

These two extremes indicate the two poles around which interpretation and formalization gravitate uneasily (as can be seen, for example, in the way psychoanalysis vacillates between a hypothesis that is functional and formal and the topical hypothesis of a 'double inscription'). The one isolates what is overstated in the phrase; the other what is unsaid. That is why logic likes to show how a single phrase in fact involves at least two propositions, while interpretative disciplines, on the other hand, show that a phrase has gaps which must be filled. Methodologically, then, it seems very difficult to stick to what is actually stated, to nothing but the *actual inscription of what is said*. Even (and above all) linguistics does not remain content with that, especially when its classifications are on a different level from what is said.

Foucault instigates a very different project: his endpoint is the statement, the simple inscription of what is said, the positivity of the dictum. Archaeology does not attempt to evade verbal performances in order to discover behind them or below their apparent surface a hidden element, a secret meaning that lies buried within them, or what emerges through them without saying so; and yet the statement is not immediately visible; it is not given in such a manifest way as a grammatical or logical struture (even if such a structure is not entirely clear, or is very difficult to elucidate). *The statement is neither visible nor hidden* [emphasis added].[21]

In these indispensable pages Foucault shows that no statement can have a latent existence, since it shows what in fact is said; even the blanks or gaps it contains must not be confused with hidden meanings [*signification*] since they indicate only the statement's presence in the space of dispersion that constitutes the 'family'. But on the other hand, if it is so difficult to find an inscription on the same level as that which is spoken, it is because the statement is not immediately perceptible but is always covered over by phrases and propositions. The 'plinth' must be discovered, polished – even fashioned or invented. The triple space of this plinth must be invented and spotlighted, and only in a multiplicity that has yet to be formed can the statement be articulated as a simple inscription of what is said. Only then does the question arise of knowing whether the interpretations and formalizations did not already presuppose this simple inscription as their precondition. In fact, is it not the inscription of the statement (the statement as inscription) which would be led under certain conditions to double up in another inscription or to project itself into a proposition? Every address [*suscription*] or subscription [*souscription*] is related to the unqiue inscription of the statement in its discursive formation: the archive as monument, not as document:

If language is to be taken as an object, decomposed into distinct levels, described and analysed, an 'enunciative datum' must exist that will always be determined and not infinite: the analysis of a language [*langue*] always operates on a corpus of words and texts; the uncovering and interpretation of implicit meanings always rests on a limited group of sentences; the logical analysis of a sytem implies a given group of propositions in the rewriting, in a formal language [*langage*].[22]

That is the essence of the concrete method. We are forced to begin with words, phrases and propositions, but we organize them into a limited corpus that varies depending on the problem raised. This requirement already lay at the heart of the 'distributionalist' school of Bloomfield or Harris. But Foucault's originality lies in the way in which he takes it upon himself to limit the different corpora which operate neither on the basis of linguistic frequency or constancy, nor according to the personal qualities of the speaker or writer (great thinkers, famous statesmen, etc.). François Ewald is right to say that Foucault's texts are 'discourses which lack a reference' and that the archivist usually avoids quoting the big names.[23] The reason is that he chooses the fundamental words, phrases and propositions not on the basis of structure or the author-subject from whom they emanate but on the basis of the simple function they carry out in a general situation: for example, the rules of internment in an asylum or even a prison; disciplinary rules in the army or at school.

Only in the books published after *Archaeology* are we given a clear reason for Foucault's choice of criteria: the words, phrases and propositions examined by the text must be those which revolve round different focal points of power (and resistance) set in play by a particular problem. For example, the question of 'sexuality' in the nineteenth century can be analysed by seeking out the words and phrases used in the confessional, or the propositions put forward by pious handbooks, as well as by examining other focal points such as schooling, or the institutions of birth, marriage, and so on.[24] This is the criterion effectively at work in the *Archaeology*, even though the theory appears only later. So once the corpus has been established (which does not in any sense impose limits on the statement) we can then determine the way in which language [*langage*] gathers round or 'falls' into this corpus. The *Order of Things* speaks of 'the being of language', while the *Archaeology* states that 'there is language' – the phrase varies in accordance with the particular approach.[25] But in each case 'one speaks' in a kind of anonymous murmur that appears in a different guise on each occasion.

It is therefore possible to isolate statements from words, phrases and propositions. Statements are not words, phrases or propositions, but rather formations thrown up by the corpus in question only when the subjects of the phrase, the objects of the proposition and the signifieds of words *change in nature*: they then occupy the place of the 'One speaks' and become dispersed throughout the opacity of language. This is a constant paradox in Foucault: the language coagulates around a corpus only in order to facilitate the distribution or dispersion of statements and to stand as the rule for a 'family' that is naturally dispersed. This whole method is carried out with the utmost rigour, and in differing degrees is applied throughout Foucault's work.

When Gogol[1] wrote his masterpiece about the inscription of dead souls, he explained that his novel was a poem and showed how and in what areas the novel must necessarily be a poem. Perhaps, in this archaeology, Foucault offers us less a discourse on his method than the poem of his previous works, and reaches the point where philosophy is necessarily poetry, the severe poetry of what is said, which subsumes both nonsense and the greatest profundities. In a certain way Foucault can declare that he has never written anything but fiction for, as we have seen, statements resemble dreams and are transformed as in a kaleidoscope, depending on the corpus in question and the diagonal line being followed. But in another sense he can also claim that he has written only what is real, and used what is real, for everything is real in the statement, and all reality in it is openly on display.

There are many multiplicities. There is not only the great dualism of discursive and non-discursive multiplicities; among the discursive elements there are also whole families or formations of statements, whose catalogue is open-ended and subject to constant change. And then there are different kinds of statements, which are distinguished by certain 'thresholds': a single family can pass through several different kinds, while one kind can incorporate several families. For example, science implies certain thresholds beyond which statements attain an 'epistemologization', a 'scientificity' or even a 'formalization'. But a science never absorbs the family or formation which defines it; the scientific status and pretensions of psychiatry cannot quell juridical texts, literary expressions, philosophical reflections, political decisions and public opinions, which all form an integral part of the corresponding discursive formation.[26] At best a science can influence the formation, by systematizing or formalizing some of its areas and being prepared to receive in turn an ideological function that cannot simply be linked to a notion of scientific imperfection.

In brief, science is concentrated in an area of knowledge it does not absorb and in a formation which is in itself the object of knowledge and not of science. Knowledge in general [*savoir*] is not science or even a particular corpus of knowledge [*connaissance*],[27] but takes as its object the above-defined multiplicities, or rather the precise multiplicity it actually describes, with all its unique features, places and functions:

> Discursive practice does not coincide with the scientific development that it may give rise to; and the knowledge that it forms is neither an unfinished prototype nor the by-product to be found in daily life of a constituted science.[28]

But one also sees, then, how certain multiplicities and formations direct the knowledge [*savoir*] haunting them not towards epistemological thresholds but in very different directions, towards completely different thresholds. We cannot simply say that certain families are 'incapable' of science, at least on the level of redistribution and real mutation (as, for example, in the case of what preceded psychiatry in the seventeenth and eighteenth centuries). Instead we wonder if there are not thresholds, for example aesthetic ones, which mobilize knowledge in a direction that is different to that of science, allowing us to offer a definition of a literary text, or a pictorial work, while remaining within the discursive practices to which they belong. There are even ethical and political thresholds, and we could show here how certain prohibitions, exclusions, limitations, freedoms and transgressions are 'linked to a particular discursive practice', related to non-discursive domains and more or less capable of approaching a revolutionary threshold.[29]

These elements lead to the formation of the archaeology-poem, made up of multiple registers, but equally of the particular inscription of an articulation linked in turn to events, institutions and all sorts of other practices. The essential point is not that we have gone beyond the duality of science and poetry that dogged the work of Bachelard, or that we have found a way of treating literary texts scientifically. Above all, what we have done is to discover and survey that foreign land where a literary form, a scientific proposition, a common phrase, a schizophrenic piece of non-sense and so on are also statements, but lack a common denominator and cannot be reduced or made equivalent in any discursive way. This is what had never before been attained by logicians, formalists or interpreters. Science and poetry are equal forms of knowledge.

But what are the limits of a family or discursive formation? How can we conceptualize the cut-off point? This is a completely different question to that of the threshold, but once again the appropriate method is not axiomatic, nor even strictly structural. For the substitution of one formation by another is not necessarily carried out at the level of the most general or most easily formalized statements. Only a serial method, as used today by historians, allows us to construct a series around a single point and to seek out other series which might prolong this point in different directions on the level of other points. There is always a point in space or time when series begin to diverge and become redistributed in a new space, and it is at this point that the break takes place.

This serial method is built up from particular features and curves. Foucault remarks that it seems to have two diametrically opposed effects, since on the one hand it encourages historians to carve history up into large periods of time, while on the other it leads epistemologists to multiply the divisions, some of which have an extremely brief duration.[30] We shall continue to come across this problem. But at all events, the essential point is that constructing series on the basis of determinable multiplicities makes it impossible to spread out history in the sequential way envisaged by those philosophers devoted to the glorification of a Subject:

> Making historical analysis the discourse of the continuous and making human consciousness the original subject of all historical development and all action are the two sides of the same system of thought. In this system, time is conceived in terms of totalization and revolutions are never more than moments of consciousness.[31]

Those who continue to have recourse to History and protest against the indetermination of a concept such as 'mutation' should bear in mind the perplexity of real historians when they have to explain why capitalism arose at such a time and in such a place when so many factors could have made it equally possible at another time and place. 'To problematize series . . .' Whether discursive or not, formations, families and multiplicities are historical. They are not just compounds built up from their coexistence but are inseparable from 'temporal reactors of derivation'; and when a new formation appears, with new rules and series, it never comes all at once, in a single phrase or act of creation, but emerges like a series of 'building blocks', with gaps, traces and reactivations of former elements that survive under the new rules. Despite isomorphisms and isotopies, no formation provides the model for another. The theory of divisions is therefore an essential part of the system.[32] One must pursue the different series, travel along the different levels, and cross all thresholds; instead of simply displaying phenomena or statements in their vertical or horizontal dimensions, one must form a transversal or mobile diagonal line along which the archaeologist-archivist must move. A comment by Boulez on the rareified universe of Webern could easily apply here to Foucault (and his style): 'He created a new dimension, which we might call a diagonal dimension, a sort of distribution of points, groups or figures that no longer act simply as an abstract framework but actually exist in space.'[33]

A New Cartographer

(Discipline and Punish)

Foucault never looked on writing as an aim or an end in itself. This is precisely what makes him a great writer and imbues everything he writes with an increasing sense of joy and gaiety. The Divine Comedy of punishment means we can retain the basic right to collapse in fits of laughter in the face of a dazzling array of perverse inventions, cynical discourses and meticulous horrors. A whole chain of phenomena, from anti-masturbation machines for children to the mechanics of prison for adults, sets off an unexpected laughter which shame, suffering or death cannot silence. The torturers rarely laugh, at least not in the same way. Vallès has already contrasted the revolutionaires' unique sense of gaiety in horror with the horrible gaiety of the torturer. Provided the hatred is strong enough something can be salvaged, a great joy which is not the ambivalent joy of hatred, but the joy of wanting to destroy whatever mutilates life.

Foucault's book is full of a joy or jubilation that blends in with the splendour of its style and the politics of its content. It is punctuated by horrible descriptions which are lovingly rendered: the botched torture of Damien; the plague-ridden city and the way it was sealed off; the chain gang passing through town calling out to people; or the new isolating machine, such as prison or the prison van, evidence of a new 'sensibility in the art of punishment'. Foucault always managed to illustrate his theatrical analyses in a vivid manner.

Here analysis becomes increasingly microphysical and the illustrations increasingly physical, expressing the 'effects' of analysis, not in a causal way but through the use of optics and colour: the red on red of the tortured inmates contrasts with the grey on grey of prison. Analysis and illustration go hand in hand, offering us a microphysics of power and a political investment of the body. These illustrations are coloured in on a minutely drawn map. This book can be taken as continuing Foucault's previous books as much as representing a decisive new step forward.

In a general or even confused way, leftism has been characterized theoretically as having raised again the problem of power, a question which has been dircted against Marxism as much as against bourgeois conceptions; and pratically as a certain form of local and specific struggle whose relationships and necessary unity could no longer come from a process of totalization or centralization, but rather, as Guattari put it, from a transversality. These two aspects, the practical and the theoretical, were closely linked. But leftism still continued to retain or reintegrate certain elements that were too basically Marxist, and once again fell back into Marxism as part of the general centralization that brought groups back to the old ways, Stalinism included. Perhaps from 1971 to 1973 the GIP (Group for Information about Prisons), under the encouragement of Foucault and Defert, managed to function in a way that avoided this resurgence by keeping up a kind of original link between prison struggle and other struggles. And when Foucault returns in 1975 to a theoretical publication he appears to be the first to invent this new conception of power, which everyone had unsuccessfully tried to find and articulate.

This is the subject matter of *Discipline and Punish*, even though Foucault touches on it only in a few pages at the beginning of his book. Only a few pages, since he adopts a method that is completely different from the 'thesis'. He is content to suggest abandoning a certain number of postulates

which have traditionally marked the position of the left.[1] And
we have to wait until *The History of Sexuality* for a more detailed
exposition.

As the postulate of property, power would be the 'property'
won by a class. Foucault shows that power does not come
about in this way: it is less a property than a strategy, and its
effects cannot be attributed to an appropriation 'but to dis-
positions, manoeuvres, tactics, techniques, functionings'; 'it is
exercised rather than possessed; it is not the "privilege",
acquired or preserved, of the dominant class, but the overall
effect of its strategic positions.' This new functionalism or
functional analysis certainly does not deny the existence of
class and class-struggle but illustrates it in a totally different
way, with landscapes, characters and behaviour that are
different from those to which traditional history, even of the
Marxist variety, has made us accustomed. We are shown
'innumerable points of confrontation, focuses of instability,
each of which has its own risks of conflict, of struggles, of an at
least temporary inversion of the power-relations.' Instead of
analogy, homology or univocality, we have a new kind of
possible continuity. In brief, power is not homogeneous but
can be defined only by the particular points through which it
passes.

As the postulate of localization, power would be power of
the State and would itself be located in the machinery of State
to the point where even 'private' powers would only apparently be dispersed and would remain no more than a special
example of the machinery of State. Foucault shows that, on
the contrary, the State itself appears as the overall effect or
result of a series of interacting wheels or structures which are
located at a completely different level, and which constitute a
'microphysics of power'. Not only private systems but explicit
parts of the machinery of State have an origin, a behaviour
and a function which the State ratifies, controls or is even
content to cover rather than institute.

One of the basic ideas in *Discipline and Punish* is that modern societies can be defined as 'disciplinarian'; but discipline cannot be identified with any one institution or apparatus precisely because it is a type of power, a technology, that traverses every kind of apparatus or institution, linking them, prolonging them, and making them converge and function in a new way. This holds even when the particular parts or wheels are as obvious a part of the State as the police or prison:

> Although the police as an institution were certainly organized in the form of a state apparatus, and although this was certainly linked directly to the centre of political sovereignty, the type of power it exercises, the mechanisms it operates and the elements to which it applies them are specific,

charging itself with forcing the discipline to penetrate right into the ephemeral detail of a social field, thereby revealing its relative independence from the judicial and even political apparatus.[2] This is all the more so since the origin of the person does not lie in the 'juridico-political structure of a society': it is wrong to make it depend on the evolution of law, even penal law. In so far as it administers punishment, prison also possesses a necessary autonomy and in turn reveals a 'disciplinary supplement' which goes beyond the machinery of State, even when used by it.[3] In brief, Foucault's functionalism throws up a new topology which no longer locates the origin of power in a privileged place, and can no longer accept a limited localization (this conception of social space, like the continuity mentioned above, is as new as that of contemporary physics and mathematics). Here we can see that 'local' has two very different meanings: power is local because it is never global, but it is not local or localized because it is diffuse.

As the postulate of subordination, this power embodied in the machinery of State would be subordinate to both a mode of production and an infrastructure. No doubt it is possible to make the great systems of punishment and the various systems of production tally: the disciplinary mechanisms in particular cannot be separated from the demographic upsurge of the eighteenth century, or a growth in production that seeks to increase yield, compose forces and extract every useful force from the body. But it is difficult to discern an economic determination 'in the last analysis', even if one endows the superstructure with the ability to react or turn back on itself. It is rather the whole economy – for example the workshop or the factory – which these mechanisms of power presuppose as they already act from within on bodies and souls, as they already act inside the economic field on the forces and relations of production: 'Relations of power are not in a position of exteriority with respect to other types of relationships . . . [they] are not in superstructural positions . . . they have a directly productive role, wherever they come into play.'[4] A functional microanalysis takes whatever is still pyramidal in the Marxist image and replaces it with a strict immanence where centres of power and disciplinary techniques form multiple segments, linked to one another which the individuals of a mass traverse or inhabit, body and soul (family, school, barracks, factory, if need be prison). The thing called power is characterized by immanence of field without transcendent unification, continuity of line without global centralization, and contiguity of parts without distinct totalization: it is a social space.[5]

As the postulate of essence or of attribute, power would have an essence and be an attribute, which would qualify those who possess it (dominators) as opposed to those on whom it is practised (dominated). Power has no essence; it is simply operational. It is not an attribute but a relation: the power-relation is the set of possible relations between forces, which passes through the dominated forces no less than through the dominating, as both these forces constitute unique elements: 'Power invests [the dominated], passes through them and with the help of them, relying on them just as they, in their struggle against power, rely on the hold it exerts on them.'

Analysing the *lettres de cachet*, Foucault demonstrates that 'the king's arbitrator' does not operate in a downward direction like an attribute of his transcendent power, but is solicited by the most humble, by the relatives, neighbours and colleagues of a nasty little troublemaker who want to have him locked up and who use the absolute monarchy like an immanent 'public service' that can settle family or conjugal arguments, professional quarrels or disputes over byways.[6] In this respect, the *lettre de cachet* therefore becomes the predecessor of what psychiatry calls a 'willing investment'. Far from operating in a general or appropriate sphere, the power-relation establishes itself wherever individual features, however tiny, are to be found: relations between forces such as 'boundary disputes, quarrels between parents and children, domestic tiffs, drunkenness and debauchery, public squabbles and a load of secret affairs'.

As the postulate of modality, power would act through the use of violence or ideology by reprimanding, by tricking or persuading, by acting as police or as propaganda. Even here, this alternative does not seem pertinent (this can clearly be seen even at a political party congress: the violence may be either in the hall or out in the street, while the ideology is always to be found on the platform; but the problem of the organization of power is settled privately in the adjoining room). Power does not come about through ideology, even when it concerns the soul; it does not necessarily separate through violence and repression, even when it weighs on the body. Or rather, violence expresses well the effect of a force on *something*, some object or being. But it does not express the power relation, that is to say the *relations between force and force*, 'an action upon an action'.[7] A relation between forces is a function of the type 'to incite, to provoke, to combine . . .'. In the case of disciplinary societies, we should say: to allocate, to classify, to compose, to normalize. The first is indefinite and varies in each case. Power 'produces reality' before it represses. Equally it produces truth before it ideologizes, abstracts or masks.[8]

By highlighting sexuality as a special case, *The History of Sexuality* will therefore show how we can believe in a sexual repression operating within language if we concentrate on words and phrases but not if we isolate the dominant statements, and especially the verbal procedures in use in churches, schools and hospitals, which simultaneously search for the reality of sex and the truth in sex. It will also show how repression and ideology explain nothing but always assume an organization or 'system' within which they operate, but not vice versa. Foucault does not in any way ignore repression and ideology; but as Nietzsche had already seen, they do not constitute the struggle between forces but are only the dust thrown up by such a contest.

As the postulate of legality State power would express itself in law, where the latter is conceived either as a state of peace imposed on brute force or as the result of a war or struggle won by the stronger party, but where in either case law is defined by the forced or voluntary cessation of war, in contrast to illegality, which it defines by way of exclusion. Here revolutionaries can only demand a different legality which comes from winning power and installing a new machinery of State. One of the strongest themes in Foucault's book consists of replacing the crude opposition of law and illegality with the subtle correlation made between *illegalisms and laws*. Law is always a structure of illegalisms, which are differentiated by being formalized. We need only look at the law of commercial societies to see that laws are not contrasted worldwide with illegality, but that some are actually used to find loopholes in others. Law administers illegalisms: some it allows, makes possible or invents as the privilege of the dominating class; others it tolerates as a compensation for the dominated classes, or even uses in the service of the dominating class; others again it forbids, isolates and takes as both its object and its means of domination.

For this reason changes in the law brought about in the

eighteenth century were ultimately designed to create a new distribution of illegalisms, not only because offences tended to change in nature, focusing increasingly on property rather than on people, but also because disciplinary powers categorized and formalized these infractions in a new way, defining a new form called 'delinquency' which in turn gave rise to a new classification and control of illegalisms.[9] Certain popular movements of resistance in the 1789 revolution can obviously be explained by the fact that the illegalisms tolerated or installed by the old regime became intolerable to republican power. But what is common to both republics and monarchies in the West is that they raised the whole entity of Law to the status of the assumed principle of power, in order to give themselves a homogeneous representation of jurisdiction: the 'juridical model' became the blueprint for all strategies.[10] This chart of illegalisms, however, continues to function according to the model of legality. And Foucault shows that the law is now no more a state of peace than the result of a successful war: it is war itself, and the strategy of this war in action, just as power is not the property of the dominant class but the strategy of that class in action.

It is as if, finally, something new were emerging in the wake of Marx. It is as if a complicity about the State were finally broken. Foucault is not content to say that we must rethink certain notions; he does not even say it; he just does it, and in this way proposes new co-ordinates for praxis. In the background a battle begins to brew, with its local tactics and overall strategies which advance not by totalizing but by relaying, connecting, converging and prolonging. The question ultimately is: *What is to be done?* The theoretical privilege given to the State as an apparatus of power to a certain extent leads to the practice of a leading and centralizing party which eventually wins State power; but on the other hand it is this very organizational conception of the party that is justified by this theory of power. The stakes of Foucault's book lie in a different theory, a different praxis of struggle, a different set of strategies.

Foucault's previous book had been *The Archaeology of Knowledge*. What kind of development does *Discipline and Punish* represent? This archaeology was not just a book of reflections or a general method but a new orientation, like a new folding acting on the earlier books. Archaeology put forward a distinction between two types of practical formations: the one 'discursive', involving statements, the other 'non-discursive', involving environment. For example, clinical medicine at the end of the eighteenth century is a discursive formation; but as such it relates to a mass and a population who depend on another kind of formation and so bring in non-discursive environments such as 'institutions, political events, economic practices and processes'. Naturally, environments also produce statements, just as statements determine environments. But the fact remains that the two formations are heterogeneous, even though they may overlap: there is no correspondence or isomorphism, no direct causality or symbolization.[11] *The Archaeology of Knowledge* therefore marked a turning point: it posited a firm distinction between the two forms but, as it proposed to define the form of statements, it contented itself with indicating the other forms in a negative way, as the 'non-discursive'.

Discipline and Punish marks a new stage. Even a 'thing' like prison is seen as an environmental formation (the 'prison' environment) and a form of content (where the content is the prisoner). But this thing or form does not refer back to a 'word' designating it, or to a signifier for which it would be the signified. It refers to completely different words and concepts, such as delinquency or delinquent, which express a new way of articulating infractions, sentences and their subjects. Let us call this formation of statements a *form of expression*. The two forms may have emerged at the same time, in the eighteenth century, but they are still none the less heterogeneous.

Penal law undergoes a development that obliges it to speak of crime and punishment in terms of the defence of society (and no longer in terms of vengeance or the restoration of sovereign power): signs addressed to the soul or mind which establish certain mental associations between the crime and the punishment (a code). But prison is a new way of acting on bodies, and evolves from something entirely different to penal law: 'Prison, that concentrated and austere figure of all the disciplines, is not an endogenous element in the penal system as defined at the turn of the eighteenth and nineteenth centuries.'[12] Penal law concerns those aspects of criminal material that can be articulated: it is a system of language that classifies and translates offences and calculates sentences; a family of statements that is also a threshold. Prison, for its part, is concerned with whatever is visible: not only does it wish to display the crime and the criminal but in itself it constitutes a visibility, it is a system of light before being a figure of stone, and is defined by 'Panopticism': by a visual assemblage and a luminous environment (a central tower surrounded by cells) in which the warder can see all the detainees without the detainees being able to see either him or one another.[13]

A system of light and a system of language are not the same form, and do not have the same formation. We begin to understand now why Foucault studies these two forms in his earlier books: the visible and the articulable, as he called them in *The Birth of the Clinic*; and, in *Madness and Civilization*, madness as seen in a general hospital and folly (which was not treated in a seventeenth-century hospital) as it is described in medicine. What *The Archaeology* recognized but still only designated negatively, as non-discursive environments, is given its positive form in *Discipline and Punish*, a form that haunted the whole of Foucault's work: the form of the visible, as opposed to the form of whatever can be articulated. For example, at the beginning of the nineteenth century masses and populations become visible, and emerge into the light of day at the same time as medical statements manage to articulate new objects (tissular lesions and the anatomo-physiological correlations).[14]

Of course, as a form of content prison itself has its own statements and regulations. Equally penal law, as a form of expression, statements of delinquency, has its contents: even if these are only a new series of offences, carried out against property rather than against people.[15] And the two forms continue to come into contact, seep into one another and steal bits for themselves: penal law still leads back to prison and provides prisoners, while prison continues to reproduce delinquency, make it an 'object', and realize the aims which penal law had conceived differently (the defence of society, the moral conversion of the condemned man, the changes made to the sentence, individuation).[16]

There is a mutual presupposition operating between the two forms, yet there is no common form, no conformity, not even correspondence. It is here that *Discipline and Punish* poses the two problems that *The Archaeology* could not raise because the latter remained tied to Knowledge, and the primacy of the statement in knowledge. On the one hand, outside forms, is there in general a common immanent cause that exists within the social field? On the other, how do the assemblages, adjustments and interpenetration of the two forms come about in a variable way in each particular case?

Form here can have two meanings: it forms or organizes matter; or it forms or finalizes functions and gives them aims. Not only the prison but the hospital, the school, the barracks and the workshop are formed matter. Punishment is a formalized function, as is care, education, training, or enforced work. The fact is that there is a kind of correspondence between them, even though the two forms are irreducible (in fact, care was not the function of the seventeenth-century hospital and the penal law in the eighteenth century does not refer essentially to prison). So how can we explain such a coadaptation? The reason lies in the fact that we can conceive of pure matter and pure functions, abstracting the forms which embody them.

When Foucault defines Panopticism, either he specifically

sees it as an optical or luminous arrangement that characterizes prison, or he views it abstractly as a machine that not
only affects visible matter in general (a workshop, barracks,
school or hospital as much as a prison) but also in general
passes through every articulable function. So the abstract
formula of Panopticism is no longer 'to see without being seen'
but *to impose a particular conduct on a particular human multiplicity*.
We need only insist that the multiplicity is reduced and
confined to a tight space and that the imposition of a form of
conduct is done by distributing in space, laying out and
serializing in time, composing in space-time, and so on.[17] The
list is endless, but it is always concerned with unformed and
unorganized matter and unformalized, unfinalized functions,
the two variables being indissolubly linked.

What can we call such a new informal dimension? On one
occasion Foucault gives it its most precise name: it is a
'diagram', that is to say a 'functioning, abstracted from any
obstacle [. . .] or friction [and which] must be detached from
any specific use'.[18] The *diagram* is no longer an auditory or
visual archive but a map, a cartography that is coextensive
with the whole social field. It is an abstract machine. It is
defined by its informal functions and matter and in terms of
form makes no distinction between content and expression, a
discursive formation and a non-discursive formation. It is a
machine that is almost blind and mute, even though it makes
others see and speak.

If there are many diagrammatic functions and even
matters, it is because every diagram is a spatio-temporal
multiplicity. But it is also because there are as many diagrams
as there are social fields in history. When Foucault invokes the
notion of diagram it is in connection with our modern disciplinarian societies, where power controls the whole field: if
there is a model it is that of the 'plague', which cordons off the
stricken town and regulates the smallest detail. But if we
consider the ancient sovereign societies we can see that they
also possess a diagram, even if it relates to different matters

and functions: here too a force is exercised on other forces, but it is used to deduct rather than to combine and compose; to divide the masses rather than to isolate the detail; to exile rather than to seal off (its model is that of 'leprosy').[19]

This is a different kind of diagram, a different machine, closer to theatre than to the factory; it involves a different relation between forces. More importantly, it creates intermediary diagrams in which we shift from one society to another: for example, the Napoleonic diagram, where the disciplinary function merges with the sovereign function 'at the point of junction of the monarchical, ritual exercise of sovereignty and the hierarchical, permanent exercise of indefinite discipline'.[20] This is because the diagram is highly unstable or fluid, continually churning up matter and functions in a way likely to create change.

Lastly, every diagram is intersocial and constantly evolving. It never functions in order to represent a persisting world but produces a new kind of reality, a new model of truth. It is neither the subject of history, nor does it survey history. It makes history by unmaking preceding realities and significations, constituting hundreds of points of emergence or creativity, unexpected conjunctions or improbable continuums. It doubles history with a sense of continual evolution.

Every society has its diagram(s). Foucault was careful to work on a well-determined series and never interested himself directly in so-called primitive societies. None the less they would be a particularly good example, perhaps too good. For far from being devoid of politics or history, they have a network of alliances which cannot be reduced to a hierarchical structure or to relations of exchange between filial groups. Alliances take place between small local groups, which constitute relations between forces (gift and counter-gift) and direct power. Here the diagram shows how it is different from structure in so far as the alliances weave a supple and transversal network that is perpendicular to vertical structure; define a practice, proceeding or strategy distinct from any single combination; and form an unstable physical system that is in perpetual disequilibrium instead of a closed, exchangist cycle (which accounts for Leach's polemic with Lévi-Strauss, or Pierre Bourdieu's sociology of strategies).

The conclusion to be drawn from this is not so much that Foucault's conception of power is particularly apt in the case of primitive societies, about which he says nothing; but that the modern societies he discusses in turn develop diagrams which expose their relations between forces or the particular strategies. In fact, within the overall categories, basic lineages or modern institutions we can still find those microrelations which, far from destroying these larger unities, actually compose them. This is precisely what Gabriel Tarde did when he founded a microsociology: he did not explain the social by reference to the individual; instead he accounted for the all-embracing categories by having recourse to minutely small relations such as 'imitation', the propagation of a current of belief or desire (quanta) or 'invention', the meeting of two imitative trends. These are the real relations between forces, in so far as they transcend mere violence.

What is a diagram? It is a display of the relations between forces which constitute power in the above conditions:

> The panoptic mechanism is not simply a hinge, a point of exchange between a mechanism of power and a function; it is a way of making power relations functions in a function, and of making a function through these power relations.[21]

We have seen that the relations between forces, or power relations, were microphysical, strategic, multipunctual and diffuse, that they determined particular features and constituted pure functions. The diagram or abstract machine is the map of relations between forces, a map of destiny, or intensity, which proceeds by primary non-localizable relations and at every moment passes through every point, 'or rather in every relation from one point to another'.[22] Of course, this has nothing to do either with a transcendent idea or with an

ideological superstructure, or even with an economic infrastructure, which is already qualified by its substance and
defined by its form and use. None the less, the diagram acts as
a non-unifying immanent cause that is coextensive with the
whole social field: the abstract machine is like the cause of the
concrete assemblages that execute its relations; and these
relations between forces take place 'not above' but within the
very tissue of the assemblages they produce.

What do we mean here by immanent cause? It is a cause
which is realized, integrated and distinguished in its effect. Or
rather the immanent cause is realized, integrated and distinguished by its effect. In this way there is a correlation or
mutual presupposition between cause and effect, between
abstract machine and concrete assemblages (it is for the
latter that Foucault most often reserves the term
'mechanisms'). If the effects realize something this is because
the relations between forces, or power relations, are merely
virtual, potential, unstable, vanishing and molecular, and
define only possibilities of interaction, so long as they do not
enter into a macroscopic whole capable of giving form to their
fluid matter and their diffuse function. But realization is
equally an integration, a collection of progressive integrations
that are initially local and then become or tend to become
global, aligning, homogenizing and summarizing relations between forces: here law is the integration of illegalisms.

The concrete assemblages of school, workshops, army,
etc., integrate qualified substances (children, workers,
soldiers) and finalized functions (education, etc.) and this
carries on right up to the State, which strives for global
integration, at least in the form of a universal Marketplace.[23]
And ultimately this realization and integration is a
differentiation: not because the cause being realized would be
a sovereign Unit, but on the contrary because the diagrammatic multiplicity can be realized and the differential of forces
integrated only by taking diverging paths, splitting into
dualisms, and following lines of differentiation without which

everything would remain in the dispersion of an unrealized cause.

Things can be realized only through doubling or dissociation, creating diverging forms among which they can then be distributed.[24] It is here, then, that we see the great dualities: between different classes, or the governing and the governed, or the public and the private. But, more than this, *it is here that two forms of realization diverge or become differentiated*: a form of expression and a form of content, a discursive and a non-discursive form, the form of the visible and the form of the articulable. It is precisely because the immanent cause, in both its matter and its functions, disregards form that it is realized on the basis of a central differentiation which, on the one hand, will form visible matter, and on the other will formalize articulable functions. Between the visible and the articulable a gap or disjunction opens up, but this disjunction of forms is the place – or 'non-place', as Foucault puts it – where the informal diagram is swallowed up and becomes embodied instead in two different directions that are necessarily divergent and irreducible. The concrete assemblages are therefore opened up by a crack that determines how the abstract machine performs.

This, then, is the reply made to the two problems posed by *Discipline and Punish*. On the one hand, the duality of forms or formations does not exclude a common, immanent cause which works informally. On the other, the common cause envisaged in each case or in each concrete mechanism will go on measuring the mixtures, captures, and interceptions taking place between elements or segments of the two forms, even though the latter are and remain irreducible and heteromorphous. It is not an exaggeration to say that every mechanism is a mushy mixture of the visible and the articulable: 'The prison system combines in a single figure discourses and architectures', programmes and mechanisms.[25] *Discipline and Punish* is the book in which Foucault expressly overcomes the apparent dualism of his earlier books (although even then this dualism was already moving towards a theory of multiplicities). If knowledge consists of linking the visible and the articulable, power is its pre-supposed cause; but, conversely, power implies knowledge as the bifurcation or differentiation without which power would not become an act: 'There is no power relation without the correlative constitution of a field of knowledge that does not presuppose and constitute at the same time power relations.'[26]

This shows up the error, even hypocrisy, that consists in thinking that knowledge appears only wherever the relations between forces are suspended. There is no model of truth that does not refer back to a kind of power, and no knowledge or even science that does not express or imply, in an act, power that is being exerted. All knowledge runs from a visible element to an articulable one, and vice versa; yet there is no such thing as a common totalizing form, not even a conformity or bi-univocal correspondence. There is only a relation of forces which acts transversally and finds in the duality of forms the conditions for its own action and realization. If there is such a thing as coadaptation of forms, it arises from their 'encounter' (provided the latter is forced), and not the other way round: 'the encounter is justified only by the new necess-ity it has established'. In this way an encounter occurs be-tween the visibilities of prison and the statements of penal law.

What is it that Foucault calls a machine, be it abstract or concrete (he speaks of the 'machine-prison', but equally of the machine-school, the machine-hospital, and so on)?[27] The con-crete machines are the two-form assemblages or mechanisms, whereas the abstract machine is the informal diagram. In other words, the machines are social before being technical. Or, rather, there is a human technology which exists before a material technology. No doubt the latter develops its effects within the whole social field; but in order for it to be even possible, the tools or material machines have to be chosen first of all by a diagram and taken up by assemblages. Historians have often been confronted by this requirement: the so-called hoplite armies are part of the phalanx assemblage; the stirrup is selected by the diagram of feudalism; the burrowing stick, the hoe and the plough do not form a linear progression but refer respectively to collective machines which vary with the density of the population and the time of the fallow.[28] In this respect, Foucault shows how the rifle exists as a tool only in the sense that it is 'a machinery whose principle would no longer be the mobile or immobile mass, but a geometry of divisible [and composable] segments'.[29]

Technology is therefore social before it is technical:

> Compared with the blast furnaces or the steam engine, panopticism has received little attention [. . .] But it would be unjust to compare the disciplinary techniques with such inventions as the steam engine [. . .] They are much less: and yet, in a way, they are much more.[30]

And if the techniques – in the narrow sense of the word – are caught within the assemblages, this is because the assemblages themselves, with their techniques, are selected by the diagrams: for example, prison can have a marginal existence in sovereign societies *(lettres de cachet)* and exists as a mechanism only when a new diagram, the disciplinary diagram, makes it cross 'the technical threshold'.[31]

It is as if the abstract and the concrete assemblages constituted two extremes, and we moved from one to the other imperceptibly. Sometimes the assemblages are distributed in hard, compact segments which are sharply separated by partitions, watertight barriers, formal discontinuities (such as school, army, workshop, and ultimately prison, and as soon as you're in the army, they tell you 'You're not at school any more'). Sometimes, on the other hand, they communicate within the abstract machine which confers on them a supple and diffuse microsegmentarity, so that they all resemble one another and prison extends throughout the rest, like the variables of the one continuous, formless function (school, barracks and the workshop are already prisons).[32]

If we continue to move from one extreme to the other, this is because each assemblage sets off the abstract machine, but in varying degrees: it resembles coefficients needed to make the diagram, and the higher the degree of variation, the more the assemblage in question becomes diffused in all the others and can suit the whole social field. Foucault's method itself here acquires a maximum flexibility. For the coefficient varies first of all from one assemblage to the next: for example, the military naval hospital is situated at the meeting-place of various circuits and sends out filters and exchangers in every direction, controlling mobilities of every sort, which make it a crossroads to a high degree, a medical space which can accommodate the complete diagram.[33] But the coefficient also varies for the same assemblage from one social field to the next, or within the same social field. Consequently, prison has three stages: in sovereign societies it exists only at the periphery of other organized forms of punishment, because it fulfils the diagram of sovereignty only to a low degree. On the other hand it becomes dispersed in every direction, and not only takes charge of the aims and penal law but impregnates the other organized forms because it fulfils to a high degree the requirements of the diagram of discipline (it still has to live down the 'bad reputation' which it gained from its previous role). And, lastly, it is doubtful whether disciplinary societies will let it keep this coefficient if in the process of development they find other ways of realizing their penal aims and of fulfilling the diagram's full range: from this we get the theme of penitentiary reform that will come increasingly to haunt the social field and ultimately deprive prison of its exemplary status, reducing it once more to the state of an assemblage that is localized, limited and separate.[34] Everything took place as if prison, like a Cartesian diver,* rose and fell on a scale

---

* (also known as Cartesian devil, or bottle imp) A device used in physics, or as a toy. A glass tube is filled with water, with an airtight membrane at the top. The tube contains a hollow object, open at the bottom, with enough water trapped to enable it to float. Pressure variations on the membrane affect the relative air density in the object, causing it to rise or fall.

gauging the degree to which the disciplinary diagram was fulfilled. There is a history of assemblages, just as there is development and change in the diagram.

This is not merely characteristic of Foucault's method but has serious consequences for his whole thought. Foucault has often been treated as above all the thinker of confinement (the general hospital in *Madness and Civilization*, the prison in *Discipline and Punish*). But this is not at all the case, and such a misinterpretation prevents us from grasping his global project. For example, Paul Virilio believes he stands in opposition to Foucault when he claims that the problem of modern societies, the problem for the 'police', is not one of confinement but concerns the 'highways', speed or acceleration, the mastery and control of speed, circuits and grids set up in open space. But this is just what Foucault has said, as is proved by the analysis of the fortress carried out by both authors, or by Foucault's analysis of the naval hospital. This misunderstanding is not serious in Virilio's case, because the force and originality of his own work testifies to the fact that encounters between independent thinkers always occur in a blind zone. On the other hand it is much more serious when less gifted authors swallow the critique whole, and either reproach Foucault for sticking to confinement, or congratulate him for having analysed it so well.

In fact, Foucault has always considered confinement a secondary element derived from a primary function that was very different in each case: there is no similarity between the way in which the general hospital or the asylum locked up madmen in the seventeenth century and the way prison locked up delinquents in the eighteenth and nineteenth centuries. The imprisonment of madmen was imposed like an 'exile' and took the leper as its model, while the confinement of delinquents was carried out by 'partitioning' and took its model from the plague victim.[35] This analysis contains some of Foucault's most beautiful pages. But exiling and partitioning are first of all precisely functions of exteriority which are only afterwards executed, formalized and organized by the mechanisms of confinement. Prison, as a hard (cellular) segmentarity refers back to a flexible and mobile function, a controlled circulation, a whole network that also crosses free areas and can learn to dispense with prison. It is a little like Kafka's 'endless procrastination' which no longer has any need of arrest or condemnation. As Maurice Blanchot says of Foucault, confinement refers to an outside, and what is confined is precisely the outside.[36] It is by excluding or placing outside that the assemblages confine something, and this holds as much for physical interiority as physical confinement. Foucault often invokes a form of the discursive, or a form of the non-discursive; but these forms neither enclose nor interiorize anything; they are 'forms of exteriority' through which either statements or visible things *are dispersed*. It is in general a question of method: instead of moving from an apparent exteriority to an essential 'nucleus of interiority' we must conjure up the illusory interiority in order to restore words and things to their constitutive exteriority.[37]

We must even distinguish between several correlative agencies, of which there are at least three. There is first of all *the outside* which exists as an unformed element of forces: the latter come from and remain attached to the outside, which stirs up their relations and draws out their diagrams. And then there is *the exterior* as the area of concrete assemblages, where relations between forces are realized. And lastly there are *the forms of exteriority*, since the realization takes place in a split or disjunction between two different forms that are exterior to one another and yet share the same assemblages (the confinements and interiorizations being only transitory figures on the surface of these forms).

Later we shall try to analyse this whole group as it appears in the form of 'the thought of the outside'. But no doubt it already shows that nothing in Foucault is really closed off. The history of forms, the archive, is doubled by an evolution of forces, the diagram. The forces appear in 'every relation from one point to another': a diagram is a map, or rather several superimposed maps. And from one diagram to the next, new maps are drawn. Thus there is no diagram that does not also include, besides the points which it connects up, certain relatively free or unbound points, points of creativity, change and resistance, and it is perhaps with these that we ought to begin in order to understand the whole picture. It is on the basis of the 'struggles' of each age, and the style of these struggles, that we can understand the succession of diagrams or the way in which they become linked up again above and beyond the discontinuities.[38] For each diagram testifies to the twisting line of the outside spoken of by Melville, without begining or end, an oceanic line that passes through all points of resistance, pitches diagrams against one another, and operates always as the most recent. And what a strange twist of the line was 1968, the line with a thousand aberrations! From this we can get the triple definition of writing: to write is to struggle and resist; to write is to become; to write is to draw a map: 'I am a cartographer'.[39]

TOPOLOGY: 'THINKING OTHERWISE'

Strata or Historical Formations: the Visible and the Articulable (Knowledge)

Strata are historical formations, positivities or empiricities. As 'sedimentary beds' they are made from things and words, from seeing and speaking, from the visible and the sayable, from bands of visibility and fields of readability, from contents and expressions. We borrow these last terms from Hjelmslev, but apply them to Foucault in a completely different way, since content is not to be confused here with a signified, nor expression with a signifier. Instead it involves a new and very rigorous division. The content has both a form and a substance: for example, the form is prison and the substance is those who are locked up, the prisoners (who? why? how?).[1] The expression also has a form and a substance: for example the form is penal law and the substance is 'delinquency' in so far as it is the object of statements. Just as penal law as a form of expression defines a field of sayability (the statements of delinquency), so prison as a form of content defines a place of visibility ('panopticism', that is to say a place where at any moment one can see everything without being seen).

This example refers us back to the earlier great analysis of strata undertaken by Foucault in *Discipline and Punish*. But it was already to be found in *Madness and Civilization*: in the classical age the asylum emerged as a place of visibility for madness, at the same time as medicine formulated basic statements about 'folly'. Between these two books Foucault published *Raymond Rouseel* and *The Birth of the Clinic*, which he wrote at the same time. The first shows how Roussel's work can be divided into two parts: visibilities invented by extraordinary machines, and statements produced by an unusual 'method'. The second book shows how, in an entirely different domain, the clinic and pathological anatomy give rise to distributions that vary between 'the visible and the articulable'.

An 'age' does not pre-exist the statements which express it, nor the visibilities which fill it. These are the two essential aspects: on the one hand each stratum or historical formation implies a distribution of the visible and the articulable which acts upon itself; on the other, from one stratum to the next there is a variation in the distribution, because the visibility itself changes in style, while the statements themselves change their system. For example, 'in the classical age' the asylum emerged as a new way of seeing and displaying madmen, a way that was very different from that of the Middle Ages or the Renaissance; while for its part medicine – but equally law, rules and regulations, literature, etc. – invented a system of statements concerning the new concept of folly. If seventeenth-century statements wrote of madness as being the last degree of folly (a key notion), then the asylum or internment envelops it in a general concept uniting madmen, vagabonds, paupers, idlers and all sorts of depraved folk: this offers a certain 'self-evidence', a historical perception or sensibility, as much as a discursive system.[2] And later, under different conditions, it is prison that provides a new way of seeing and displaying crime, and delinquency a new way of saying.

A way of saying and seeing, discursive practices and forms of self-evidence: each stratum is a combination of the two, and in the move from one stratum to the next they vary in terms of composition and combination. What Foucault takes from History is that determination of visible and articulable features unique to each age which goes beyond any behaviour, mentality or set of ideas, since it makes these things possible. But History responds only because Foucault has managed to invent, no doubt in a way related to the new conceptions of certain historians, a properly philosophical form of interrogation which is itself new and which revives History.

It is *The Archaeology of Knowledge* which will draw out the methodological conclusions and present the generalized theory of the two elements of stratification: the articulable and the visible, the discursive formations and the non-discursive formations, the forms of expression and the forms of content. This book, however, seems to grant the statement a radical primacy. The bands of visibility are now designated only in a negative way, as 'non-discursive formations' situated in a space which is complementary only to a field of statements. Foucault states that discursive relations exist between the discursive statement and the non-discursive. But he never says whether the non-discursive can be reduced to a statement, and whether or not it is a residue or an illusion. The question of primacy is essential: the statement has primacy, and we shall see why. But primacy has never meant reduction. Throughout the entire range of Foucault's work, visibilities will remain irreducible to statements and remain all the more so for developing a passion for the action of statements.

The subtitle of *The Birth of the Clinic* was 'An Archaeology of the Gaze'. It is not enough to say that Foucault denounced this subtitle, as he always corrected his previous books, unless we ask ourselves why and on what issue. Now the issue involved here is obviously the question of primacy. Foucault believes more and more that his earlier books do not sufficiently show primacy of the systems of a statement over the different ways of seeing or perceiving. This is his reaction against phenomenology. But for him, the primacy of statements will never impede the historical irreducibility of the visible – quite the contrary, in fact. The statement has

primacy only because the visible has its own laws, an autonomy that links it to the dominant, the heautonomy of the
statement. It is because the articulable has primacy that the
visible contests it with its own form, which allows itself to be
determined without being reduced. In Foucault, the places of
visibility will never have the same rhythm, history or form as
the fields of statements, and the primacy of the statement will
be valuable only in this way, to the extent that it brings itself
to bear on something irreducible.

If we forget the theory of visibilities we distort Foucault's
conception of history, but equally we distort his thought and
his conception of thought in general. We make it into a
variation of contemporary analytical philosophy, with which
he has little in common (with the possible exception of
Wittgenstein, if we isolate in the latter an original link between the visible and the articulable). Foucault continued to
be fascinated by what he saw as much as by what he heard or
read, and the archaeology he conceived of is an audiovisual
archive (beginning with the history of science). Foucault de-
lighted in articulating statements and in distinguishing between them, only because he also had a passion for seeing:
what defines him above all is the voice, but also the eyes. The
eyes and the voice. Foucault never stopped being a *voyant* at
the same time as he marked philosophy with a new style of
statement, though the two followed different paths, or a
double rhythm.

The stratified element is not the indirect object of a
knowledge which would subsequently emerge but instead
something that directly constitutes a knowledge: the lesson of
things *and* the lesson of grammar. This is why the strata are
the affair of archaeology, precisely because archaeology does
not necessarily refer back to the past. There is an archaeology
of the present. Present or past, the visible is like the
articulable: they are the object not of a phenomenology, but of
an epistemology. What Foucault will reproach in *Madness and
Civilization* is the desire to continue to invoke an experience

lived as raw or savage, in the manner of the phenomen-
ologists, or the eternal values of the imagination, as in the case
of Bachelard. But in fact there is nothing prior to knowledge,
because knowledge, in Foucault's new concept of it, is defined
by the combinations of visible and articulable that are unique
to each stratum or historical formulation. Knowledge is a
practical assemblage, a 'mechanism' of statements and
visibilities. There is therefore nothing behind knowledge
(although, as we shall see, there are things outside
knowledge). That is to say that knowledge exists only
according to certain widely varying 'thresholds' which impose
particular layers, splits and directions on the stratum in
question. In this respect, it is not enough to speak of a
'threshold of epistemologization': the latter is already moving
in a direction that leads to science, and will still cross a
threshold of 'scientificity' and ultimately a 'threshold of formalization'. But other thresholds, moving off in other directions, also leave their mark on the stratum: thresholds involving ethics, aesthetics, politics, etc.[3]

Knowledge is not science and cannot be separated from the
various thresholds in which it is caught up, including even the
experience of perception, the values of the imagination, the
prevailing ideas or commonly held beliefs. Knowledge is the
unity of stratum which is distributed throughout the different
thresholds, the stratum itself existing only as the stacking-up
of these thresholds beneath different orientations, of which
science is only one. There are only practices, or positivities,
which are constitutive of knowledge: the discursive practices
of statements, or the non-discursive practices of visibilities.
But these practices still exist beneath archaeological
thresholds whose shifting points of demarcation constitute the
historical differences between strata. This is Foucault's positivism or pragmatism; and he has never had any problem
concerning the links between science and literature, or the
imaginary and the scientific, or the known and the lived,
because the conception of knowledge impregnated and

mobilized every threshold by making each one into the variable of the stratum which stood as a historical formation.

Of course, things and words are very vague terms with which to designate the two poles of knowledge, and Foucault will go on to say that the title *Les mots et les choses*[4] should be taken ironically. The task of archaeology is firstly to discover a true form of expression which cannot be confused with any linguistic study, be it signifier, word, phrase, proposition, or linguistic act. In particular, Foucault lays into the Signifier, where 'discourse is annihilated in its reality by entering into the order of the signifier.'[5] We have seen how Foucault discovered the form of expresson in a most original conception of the 'statement' which viewed it as a function that crosses different unities, tracing a diagonal line more akin to music than to a signifying system. We must therefore break open words, phrases or propositions and extract statements from them, as Raymond Roussel did when he invented his 'method'. But a similar operation is necessary for the form of content; the latter is no more a signified than an expression is a signifier. Nor is it a state of things, or a referent. Visibilities are not to be confused with elements that are visible or more generally perceptible, such as qualities, things, objects, compounds of objects. In this respect Foucault constructs a function that is no less original than that of the statement. We must break things open. Visibilities are not forms of objects, nor even forms that would show up under light, but rather forms of luminosity which are created by the light itself and allow a thing or object to exist only as a flash, sparkle or shimmer.[6]

This is the second element which Foucault isolates in Raymond Roussel, or which perhaps he also tried to isolate in Manet. And if the conception of the statement seemed to be inspired by music and owe more to Webern than to linguistics, the conception of the visible seems pictorial, close to Delaunay, for whom light was a form that created its own forms and movements. Delaunay used to say that Cézanne broke the fruit-bowl, and we should not try to stick it back together again, like the Cubists. Like Roussel's enterprise, the task of archaeology is double: it must *open up* words, phrases and propositions, *open up* qualities, things and objects. It must extract from words and language the statements corresponding to each stratum and its thresholds, but equally extract from things and sight the visibilities and 'self-evidences' unique to each stratum.

Why these necessary extractions? Let us begin with statements: they are never hidden, yet are not directly readable or even sayable. One might think sometimes that statements are often hidden, because they are disguised, withheld or even repressed. But beyond the fact that this implies a false conception of Power, it holds only if we stick to words, phrases and propositions. This is what Foucault shows in sexuality, from the opening pages of *The History of Sexuality*: we may think that in the Victorian age a whole vocabulary was banned, phrases were metaphorized and language refined, so that sexuality could remain the ultimate secret betrayed only by reckless damned souls until Freud came on the scene, but this is not at all the case, for never was a stratum or historical formation more teeming with statements of sexuality, determining its conditions, systems, places, occasions and interlocutors (to which psychoanalysis will later add its own). We would misunderstand the role of the Church after the Council of Trent if we did not follow up this proliferation of sexual discourses:

> Under the authority of a language that had been carefully expurgated so that it was no longer directly named, sex was taken charge of, tracked down as it were, by a discourse that aimed to allow it no obscurity, no respite [. . .] What is peculiar to modern societies, in fact, is not that they consigned sex to a shadow existence, but that they dedicated themselves to speaking of it *ad infinitum*, while explaining it as *the* secret.[7]

In brief, the statement does remain hidden, but only if we do not rise to its extractive conditions; on the contrary, it is there and says everything as soon as we reach these conditions. The same holds true for politics: politics hides nothing, in diplomacy, legislation, control or government, even though each cluster of statements assumes a certain method for inter-twining words, phrases and propositions. We need only know how to read, however difficult that may prove to be. The secret exists only in order to be betrayed, or to betray itself. Each age articulates perfectly the most cynical elements of its politics, or the rawest element of its sexuality, to the point where transgression has little merit. Each age says everything it can according to the conditions laid down for its statements.

From *Madness and Civilization* on, Foucault analysed the discourse of the 'philanthropist' who freed madmen from their chains, without concealing the more effective set of chains to which he destined them.[8] That everything is always said in every age is perhaps Foucault's greatest historical principle: behind the curtain there is nothing to see, but it was all the more important each time to describe the curtain, or the base, since there was nothing either behind or beneath it. By objecting that there are statements which are hidden, we are merely stating that there are locutors and addressees who vary depending on the systems or conditions. But locutors and addressees are only some of the variables of the statement, and depend greatly on the conditions which define the statement itself as a function.

In brief, the statements become readable or sayable only in relation to the conditions which make them so and which constitute their single inscription on an 'enunciative base' (we have seen that there were not two inscriptions, the one apparent and the other hidden). This single inscription, the form of expression, is created from the statement and its conditions, the base or the curtain. Foucault presents a theatre of statements, or a sculpture made from articulable elements, 'monuments' and not 'documents'.

What is the most general condition of statements or discursive formations? Foucault's reply is all the more important for excluding in advance any subject of enunciation. The subject is a variable, or rather a set of variables of the statement. It is a function derived from the primitive function, or from the statement itself. *The Archaeology of Knowledge* analyses this subject- function: the subject is a place or position which varies greatly according to its type and the threshold of the statement, and the 'author' himself is merely one of these possible positions in certain cases. A single statement can even have several positions. So much so that what comes first is a ONE SPEAKS, an anonymous murmur in which positions are laid out for possible subjects: 'the great relentless disordered drone of discourse'.

At several instances Foucault invokes this great murmur, within which he even wishes to place himself.[9] He challenges three different ways of making language begin: the use of persons, even if these are only linguistic or used simply to get things moving (linguistic personology, the 'I speak' against which Foucault constantly puts forward the pre-existence of the third person as a non-person); or the use of the signifier which acts as the internal organization or first direction to which language refers (linguistic structuralism, the 'it speaks' against which Foucault sets the pre-existence of a given body or set of specific statements); or else the idea of an original experience, a first complicity with the world which for us would form the basis of being able to speak about it, and would make the visible the basis of the articulable (phenomenology, the 'World speaks', as if visible things already murmured a meaning which our language had only to take up, or as if language backed on to an expressive silence, against which Foucault sets up a difference in nature between seeing and speaking).[10]

Language is offered up in its entirety, or not at all. What, then, are the conditions of the statement? It is offered up by the 'there is language', 'the being of language' or the language-being, that is to say by the dimension involved, which is not to be confused with any of the directions to which language refers:

> Ignore its power to designate, to name, to show, to reveal, to be the place of meaning or truth, and, instead, turn one's attention to the moment – which is at once solidified, caught up in the play of the 'signifier' and the 'signified' – that determines its unique and limited existence.[11]

But what exactly gives a concrete meaning to Foucault's thesis, what stops it from falling into a generally phenomenological or linguistic direction, which allows it to invoke a unique and limited existence? Foucault is close to 'distributionalism', and after the publication of *The Archaeology of Knowledge* he always begins with a specific and finite body of words and texts, phrases and propositions. In this way he seeks to isolate their enunciative 'regularities', for however much they may differ, they are all produced in the same age.

From this point on the conditions, or *a priori* of the statement, are themselves historical: the great murmur, otherwise known as the language-being or the 'there is' of language, varies in each historical formation and, while being anonymous, is none the less unique, the 'enigmatic and precarious being' which cannot be separated from a particular mode. Each age has its own particular way of putting language together, because of its different groupings. For example, if in the clasasical age the being of language appears completely within the limits of representation it lays down, by the nineteenth century it leaps out of its representative functions: it is now on the point of losing its unifying function, but only in order to rediscover it elsewhere in a different mode, in literature which acts as a new function ('man had been a figure occurring between two modes of language').[12] Therefore the historical being of language never manages to gather this new function in an inner consciousness that founds, originates or even mediates; on the contrary, it constitutes a form of exteriority in which the statements of the corpus under consideration appear by way of dispersal and dissemination. It is a distributive unity. 'The *a priori* of positivities is not only the system of a temporal dispersion; it is itself a transformable group.'[13]

Everything which has just been said about the statement and its conditions must also be said about visibility. For if, in their turn, visibilities are never hidden, they are none the less not immediately seen or visible. They are even invisible so long as we consider only objects, things or perceptible qualities, and not the conditions which open them up. And if things close up again afterwards, visibilities become hazy or blurred to the point where 'self-evident' phenomena cannot be grasped by another age: when the classical age lumped together madmen, vagabonds and the unemployed, 'what for us is merely a vague sensibility was for the classical man most certainly a clearly set-out perception'. However, the conditions pertaining to visibility are not the way in which a subject sees: the subject who sees is himself a place within visibility, a function derived from visibility (as in the place of the king in classical representation, or the place of any observer in any prison system).

Must we then invoke imaginary values which would give direction to perception, or sets of perceptible qualities which would constitute 'perceptive themes'? This would be the dynamic image or quality which would constitute the conditions for the visible element, and Foucault in *Madness and Civilization* sometimes sounds like Bachelard.[14] But he soon reaches another solution. If different examples of architecture, for example, are visibilities, places of visibilities, this is because they are not just figures of stone, assemblages of things and combinations of qualities, but first and foremost forms of light that distribute light and dark, opaque and transparent, seen and non-seen, etc. In one famous section, *The Order of Things* describes Velásquez's painting *Las Meninas* as a system of light that opens up the space of classical representation and distributes what is seen and who sees, the exchanges and reflections, right up to the place of the king who can only be inferred as existing outside the painting (didn't the destroyed manuscript on Manet describe a completely different system of light, with a different use of the mirror and a different distribution of reflections?).

For its part, *Discipline and Punish* describes prison architecture, the Panopticon, as a luminous form that bathes the peripheral cells in light but leaves the central tower opaque, distributing prisoners who are seen without being able to see, and the observer who sees everything without being seen. As statements are inseparable from systems, so visibilities are inseparable from machines. A machine does not have to be optical; but it is an assembly of organs and functions that makes something visible and conspicuous (the 'machine-prison' or Roussel's machines). Foucault had provided a general formula for this as early as *Raymond Roussel*: a first light opens up things and brings forth visibilities as flashes and shimmerings, which are the 'second light'.[15] And *The Birth of the Clinic* could adopt the subtitle: 'An Archaeology of the Gaze' to the extent that each historical medical formation modulated a first light and constituted a space of visibility for illness, making symptoms gleam, either like the clinic by unfolding things in two dimensions, or like pathology by refolding them, using a third dimension that restores depth to the eye and volume to pain (illness here being an 'autopsy' of the living).

Therefore there is a 'there is' of light, a being of light or a light-being, just as there is a language-being. Each of them is an absolute and yet historical, since each is inseparable from the way in which it falls into a formation or corpus. The one makes visibilities visible or perceptible, just as the other made statements articulable, sayable or readable. This holds true to such an extent that visibilities are neither the acts of a seeing subject nor the data of a visual meaning (Foucault later denounced the subtitle: 'An Archaeology of the Gaze'). Just as the visible cannot be reduced to a perceptible thing or quality, so the light-being cannot be reduced to a physical environment: Foucault is closer to Goethe than to Newton. The light-being is a strictly indivisible condition, an *a priori* that is uniquely able to lay visibilities open to sight, and by the same stroke to the other senses, each time according to certain combinations which are themselves visible: for example, the tangible is a way in which the visible hides another visible. What *The Birth of the Clinic* had already uncovered was an 'absolute gaze', a 'virtual visibility', a 'visibility outside the gaze', which dominated all perceptible experiences and did not summon up sight without also summoning the other fields of perception, hearing and touch.[16]

Visibilities are not defined by sight but are complexes of actions and passions, actions and reactions, multisensorial complexes, which emerge into the light of day. As Magritte says in a letter to Foucault, thought is what sees and can be described visibly. Must we then relate this first light in Foucault to Heidegger's *Lichtung* or to Merleau-Ponty, a free or open element that addresses itself to sight only secondarily? There are two points of difference: Foucault's light-being is inseparable from a particular mode, and while being *a priori* is none the less historical and epistemological rather than phenomenological; on the other hand it is not as open to the word as to sight, since the word as statement finds completely different conditions for such an opening in the language-being and its historical modes.

The conclusion we can draw is that each historical formation sees and reveals all it can within the conditions laid down for visibility, just as it says all it can within the conditions relating to statements. Nothing is every secret, even though nothing is ever immediately visible or directly readable. And in both cases the conditions do not meet deep within a consciousness or a subject, any more than they compose a single Entity: they are two forms of exteriority within which dispersion and dissemination take place, sometimes of statements, sometimes of visibilities. Language 'contains' words, phrases and propositions, but does not contain statements which are disseminated in accordance with certain irreducible distances. Statements are dispersed in accordance with their threshold and family. This applies equally to light, which contains objects, but not visibilities. Equally, as we have seen, it is a mistake to think that Foucault is interested in the environments of enclosure as such: hospitals and prisons are first and foremost places of visibility dispersed in a form of exteriority, which refer back to an extrinsic function, that of setting one apart and controlling . . .

It is neither a history of mentality, nor of behaviour. Speaking and seeing, or rather statements and visibilities, are pure Elements, *a priori* conditions under which all ideas are formulated and behaviour displayed, at some moment or other. This research into conditions constitutes a sort of neo-Kantianism unique to Foucault. However, Foucault differs in certain fundamental respects from Kant: the conditions are those of real experience (statements, for example, assume a limited corpus); they are on the side of the 'object' and historical formation, not a universal subject (the *a priori* itself is historical); all are forms of exteriority.[17] But if there is any neo-Kantianism, it is because visibilities together with their conditions form a Receptivity, and statements together with their conditions form a Spontaneity. The spontaneity of language and the receptivity of light. Therefore it was not enough to equate receptive with passive and spontaneous with active. Receptive does not mean passive, since there is as much action as passion in whatever light reveals. Spontaneous does not mean active, but rather the activity of an 'Other' which acts upon the receptive form. This was already so in Kant, where the spontaneity of the 'I think' acted on receptive beings who necessarily represented this spontaneity to themselves as something other.[18]

In Foucault, the spontaneity of understanding, the *Cogito*, gives way to the spontaneity of language (the 'there is' of language), while the receptivity of intuition gives way to that of light (a new form of space-time). Henceforth it is easy to understand why the statement has a primacy over the visible: *The Archaeology of Knowledge* can claim a *determining* role for statements as discursive formations. But visibilities are no less irreducible, because they refer to a form of the *determinable*, which refuses to be reduced to the form of determination. This marked the point of Kant's decisive break with Descartes: the form of determination (I think) does not rest on an undetermined element (I am) but rather on the form of a pure determinable element (space-time). The problem is that of the coadaptation of the two forms or two sorts of conditions, which differ in nature. It is a transformed version of this problem which we find in Foucault: the relationship between the two forms of 'there is', between light and language, determinable visibilities and determining statements.

From the beginning, one of Foucault's fundamental theses is the following: there is a difference in nature between the form of content and the form of expression, between the visible and the articulable (although they continually overlap and spill into one another in order to compose each stratum or form of knowledge). Perhaps this is the first area in which Foucault encounters Blanchot: 'speaking is not seeing'. But while Blanchot insisted on the primacy of speaking as a determining element, Foucault, contrary to what we might think at first glance, upholds the specificity of seeing, the irreducibility of the visible as a determinable element.[19]

Between the two there is no isomorphism or conformity, in spite of a mutual presupposition and the primacy of the statement. Even *The Archaeology of Knowledge*, which insists on the primacy, will state that there is neither causality from the one to the other nor symbolization between the two, and that if the statement has an object, it is a discursive object which is unique to the statement and is not isomorphic with the visible object. Of course we can always *dream* of isomorphism, either in the form of an epistemological dream – as when the clinic affirms a structural identity 'between the visible and the articulable', the symptom and the sign, the spectacle and the words – or in the form of an aesthetic dream, as when a 'calligram' gives the same form to both text and drawing, to the linguistic and the plastic, to the statement and the image.[20]

In his commentary on Magritte, Foucault shows that there will always be a resurgence of 'the little thin band, colourless and neutral' separating text from figure, the drawing of the pipe from the statement 'this is a pipe' to the point where the statement becomes 'this *is not* a pipe', since neither the drawing, nor the statement, nor the 'this' as an apparently common form is a pipe: 'the drawing of the pipe and the text that ought to name it cannot find a place to meet, either on the black canvas or above it.' It is a 'non-relation'.[21]

Perhaps it is the humorous version of a process which Foucault had initiated in his historical studies. For *Madness and Civilization* showed just this: that the general hospital as a form of content or a place of visibility for madness did not have its origins in medicine, but in the police; while medicine as a form of expression, an agent of production for statements of 'folly', deployed its discursive system, its diagnoses and its treatment, outside the hospital. Commenting on Foucault, Maurice Blanchot will call this a difference or a confrontation *between* folly and madness. *Discipline and Punish* will take up and develop a neighbouring theme, in which prison as the visibility of crime does not derive from penal law as a form of expression but evolves from something completely different, which is 'disciplinary' and not judicial; while penal law, for its part, produces its statements of 'delinquency' independently of prison, as though it were always led to say, in a certain way, that this *is not* a prison . . . The two forms do not have the same formation, genesis or genealogy, in the archaeological sense of *Gestaltung*. Yet they do meet, even if it is the result of a certain 'jiggery-pokery': we might say that prison substitutes another person for the penal delinquent and, as a result of this substitution, produces or reproduces delinquency, at the same time as the law produces and reproduces prisoners.[22] Between the two alliances are formed and broken, and there is occasional overlapping on particular strata and thresholds. How can we explain that, for Foucault as for Blanchot, the non-relation is still a relation, even one of a deeper sort?

We can say, in fact, that there are 'games of truth', or rather procedures for truth. Truth is inseparable from the procedure establishing it (*Discipline and Punish* will compare the 'inquisitorial enquiry' model of science and nature prevalent at the end of the Middle Ages with the 'disciplinary examination' model of the human sciences to be found at the end of the eighteenth century). But what constitutes a procedure? Perhaps it is a pragmatism, broadly made up of a process and a method. The process is that of seeing, and poses a series of questions for knowledge: what does one see on such and such a stratum or threshold?

We are not asking only about the objects with which we begin, the qualities we follow and the states of things in which we are located (a perceptible corpus), but also how can we extract visibilities from these objects, qualities and things, how do these visibilities shimmer and gleam and under what light, and how does this light gather on the stratum? Furthermore, what are the variable subject-positions of these visibilities? Who occupies and sees them? But there are also methods of language, as different from one stratum to the next as they are from one unusual author to the next (for example, propositions).[23] How can we extract from them the 'statements' which traverse them? What system of language is used to disperse these statements, what families and thresholds are involved? And who speaks, that is to say who are the variables, the subjects of the statements, and who fills that place? In brief, there are enunciative methods and machine-like processes.

This whole range of questions on every occasion constitutes

the problem of truth. *The Use of Pleasure* will draw out the conclusions of all the earlier books when it shows that truth offers itself to knowledge only through a series of 'problematizations' and that these problematizations are created only on the basis of 'practices', practices of seeing and speaking.[24] These practices, the process and the method, constitute the procedures for truth, 'a history of truth'. But these two halves of truth must enter into a relation, problematically, at the very moment when the problem of truth denies any possible correspondence or conformity between them.

To take a very summary example, in psychiatry: is the man we see in the asylum and the man we can label mad ever one and the same? For example, it is easy to 'see' the paranoic madness of President Schreber, and to put him in the asylum, but then we have to take him out again because it is much more difficult to go on to 'articulate' his madness. On the other hand it is easy to articulate the madness of a monomaniac, but it is very difficult to see it in time and to intern him when we ought.[25] Many people are in the asylum who ought not to be there, but many are also not there who ought to be: psychiatry in the nineteenth century is built on this observation which, far from forming a solid univocal concept of madness, 'problematizes' it.

Truth is defined neither by conformity or common form, nor by a correspondence between the two forms. There is a disjunction between speaking and seeing, between the visible and the articulable: 'what we see never lies in what we say', and vice versa. The conjunction is impossible for two reasons: the statement has its own correlative object and is not a proposition designating a state of things or a visible object, as logic would have it; but neither is the visible a mute meaning, a signified of power to be realized in language, as phenomenology would have it. The archive, the audiovisual is disjunctive. So it is not surprising that the most complete examples of the disjunction between seeing and speaking are to be found in the cinema. In the Straubs, in Syberberg, in

Marguerite Duras, the voices emerge, on the one hand, like a 'story/history' [*histoire*] without a place, while the visible element, on the other hand, presents an empty place without a story/history.[26]

In Marguerite Duras's *India Song*, voices evoke or revive a ball in the past which will never be shown, while the visual image shows another ball, in silence, without any flashback making a visible link or any voice-off a sound link; while, even earlier, *La femme du Gange* was made up from two films, 'the film of the image and the film of the voices', a void being the only 'linking factor', one that simultaneously acts as a hinge and a crack. Between the two there is a perpetual irrational break. And yet they are not any old voices on top of any old images. Of course, there is no link that could move from the visible to the statement, or from the statement to the visible. But there is a continual relinking which takes place over the irrational break or the crack.

It is in this sense that the visible and the statement form a stratum, one that is none the less continually crossed and constituted by a central archaeological fissure (Straub). As long as we stick to things and words we can believe that we are speaking of what we see, that we see what we are speaking of, and that the two are linked: in this way we remain on the level of an empirical exercise. But as soon as we open up words and things, as soon as we discover statements and visibilities, words and sight are raised to a higher exercise that is *a priori*, so that each reaches its own unique limit which separates it from the other, a visible element that can only be seen, an articulable element that can only be spoken. And yet the unique limit that separates each one is also the common limit that links one to the other, a limit with two irregular faces, a blind word and a mute vision. Foucault is uniquely akin to contemporary film.

How, then, is the non-relation a relation? Or, rather, is there a contradiction between these two statements by Foucault: on the one hand, it is in vain that we say what we see; what we see never resides in what we say. And it is in vain that we attempt to show, by the use of images, metaphors, or similes, what we are saying; the space where they achieve their splendour is not that deployed by our eyes but that defined by the sequential elements or syntax;

on the other,

between the figure and the text we must admit a whole series of crisscrossings, or rather between the one and the other attacks are launched and arrows fly against the enemy target, campaigns designed to undermine and destroy, wounds and blows from the lance, a battle . . . images falling into the midst of words, verbal flashes crisscrossing drawings . . . discourse cutting into the form of things,

and vice versa.[27] The two sorts of text do not in the least contradict each other. The first says that there is no isomorphism or homology, nor any common form to seeing and speaking, to the visible and the articulable. The second says that the two forms spill over into one another, as in a battle. The image of a battle signifies precisely that there is no isomorphism. The two heterogeneous forms comprise a condition and a conditioned element, light and visibilities, language and statements; however, the condition does not 'contain' the conditioned element but offers it in a space of dissemination, and offers up itself as a form of exteriority. Therefore, it is between the visible and its conditions that statements glide, as with Magritte's two pipes. It is between the statement and its conditions that visibilities insinuate themselves, as in Roussel, who does not open up words without forcing something of the visible to emerge (and who equally does not open up things without forcing something of the statement to emerge).

We tried to show earlier how the form of visibility known as 'prison' engendered second-degree statements which reintroduced delinquency, even if this means that penal statements engender second-degree visible elements which reinforce prison. Moreover, it is the statements and visibilities which grapple like fighters, force one another to do something or capture one another, and on every occasion constitute 'truth'. This accounts for Foucault's formula: 'to speak and to show in a simultaneous motion . . . [a] prodigious . . . inter-weaving'.[28] Speaking and seeing *at the same time*, although it is not the same thing, although we do not speak of what we see, or see that of which we speak. But the two comprise the stratum, and from one stratum to the next are transformed at the same time (although not according to the same rules).

All the same, this first response (struggle, grappling, battle, double insinuation) is not enough. It does not take account of the primacy of the statement. The statement has primacy by virtue of the spontaneity of its conditions (language) which give it a determining form, while the visible element, by virtue of the receptivity of its conditions (light), merely has the form of the determinable. Therefore, we can assume that determination always comes from the statement, although the two forms differ in nature. This is why Foucault singles out a new element in the work of Roussel: not only does it open things up in order to induce statements, or open words up in order to conduct visibiliites, but it makes statements blossom and proliferate, by virtue of their spontaneity, in such a way that they exert an infinite determination over the visible element.[29] In brief, this is a second response to the problem of the relation between the two forms: only statements are determining and revelatory, even though they reveal something other than what they say. We are not surprised that in *The Archaeology of Knowledge* the visible is now more or less designated only negatively, as the non-discursive, but that the discursive has even more discursive relations with the non-discursive. Between the visible and the articulable we must maintain all the following aspects at the same time: the heterogeneity of the two forms, their difference in nature or anisomorphism; a mutual presupposition between the two, a mutual grappling and capture; the well-determined primacy of the one over the other.

Even so, this second response is still not enough. If determination is infinite how would the determinable element not be inexhaustible, since it would have a different form to that of determination? How would the visible not slip away, as something eternally determinable, when statements can determine it *ad infinitum*? How can we stop the object from escaping? Is it not on this point that Roussel's work finally runs aground, not in the general sense of failure, but in the strictly naval sense?:

> Now language is arranged in a circle within itself, hiding what it has to show, flowing at a dizzying speed toward an invisible void where things are beyond reach and where it disappears on its mad pursuit of them.[30]

Kant had already undergone a similar adventure: the spontaneity of understanding did not exert its determination on the receptivity of intuition without the latter continuing to contrast its form of the determinable with that of determination. Kant therefore had to invoke a third agency beyond the two forms that was essentially 'mysterious' and capable of taking account of their coadaptation as Truth. This was the *schema* of imagination. The word 'enigmatic' in Foucault corresponds to mystery in Kant, although it is part of a completely different whole and distributed differently.

But even Foucault needs a third agency to coadapt the determinable and determination, the visible and the articulable, the receptivity of light and the spontaneity of language, operating either beyond or this side of the two forms. It is for this reason that Foucault said that the grappling implies a *distance* across which the adversaries 'exchange their threats and words', and that the place of confrontation implies a 'non-place' which bears witness to the fact that the opponents do not belong to the same space or rely on the same form.[31] In the same way, analysing Paul Klee,

Foucault says that the visible figures and the signs of writing combine, *but in a different dimension to that of their respective forms.*[32] In this way we must also leap into a different dimension to that of the stratum and its two forms, a third informal dimension that will take account both of the stratified composition of the two forms and of the primacy of the one over the other. What comprises this dimension, this new axis?

Strategies or the Non-stratified: the Thought of the Outside (Power)

What is Power? Foucault's definition seems a very simple one: power is a relation between forces, or rather every relation between forces is a 'power relation'. In the first place we must understand that power is not a form, such as the State-form; and that the power relation does not lie between two forms, as does knowledge. In the second place, force is never singular but essentially exists in relation with other forces, such that any force is already a relation, that is to say power: force has no other object or subject than force. This does not create a return to natural law, because for its part law is a form of expression, whereas Nature is a form of visibility *and violence a concomitance or consequence of force, but not a constituent element.* Foucault is closer to Nietzsche (and to Marx), for whom the relation between forces greatly exceeds violence and cannot be defined by the latter. Violence acts on specific bodies, objects or beings whose form it destroys or changes, while force has no object other than that of other forces, and no being other than that of relation: it is 'an action upon an action, on existing actions, or on those which may arise in the present or future'; it is 'a set of actions upon other actions'. We can therefore conceive of a necessarily open list of variables expressing a relation between forces or power relation, constituting actions upon actions: to incite, to induce, to seduce, to make easy or difficult, to enlarge or limit, to make more or less probable, and so on.[1]

These are the categories of power. In this sense, *Discipline and Punish* had established a more detailed list of the values which the relation between forces assumed in the course of the eighteenth century: *distribution in space* (which took concrete form in enclosing, controlling, arranging, placing in series . . .), *ordering in time* (subdividing time, programming an action, decomposing a gesture . . .), *composition in space-time* (the various ways of 'constituting a productive force whose effect had to be superior to the sum of elementary forces that composed it'), and so on.[2] This is why Foucault's great theses on power, as seen above, develop under three headings: power is not essentially repressive (since it 'incites, it induces, it seduces'); it is practised before it is possessed (since it is possessed only in a determinable form, that of class, and a determined form, that of State); it passes through the hands of the mastered no less than through the hands of the masters (since it passes through every related force). A profound Nietzscheanism.

Therefore we should not ask: 'What is power and where does it come from?', but 'How is it practised?' An exercise of power shows up as an affect, since force defines itself by its very power to affect other forces (to which it is related) and to be affected by other forces. To incite, provoke and produce (or any term drawn from analogous lists) constitute active affects, while to be incited or provoked, to be induced to produce, to have a 'useful' effect, constitute reactive affects. The latter are not simply the 'repercussion' or 'passive side' of the former but are rather 'the irreducible encounter' between the two, especially if we believe that the force affected has a certain capacity for resistance.[3] At the same time, each force has the power to affect (others) and to be affected (by others again), such that each force implies power relations: and every field of forces distributes forces according to these relations and their variations. Spontaneity and receptivity now take on a new meaning: to affect or to be affected.

The power to be affected is like a *matter* of force, and the power to affect is like a *function* of force. But it is a pure function, that is to say a non-formalized function, independent of the concrete forms it assumes, the aims it serves and the means it employs: as a physics of action, it is a physics of abstract action. And it is also a pure unformed matter independent of the formed substances, qualified objects or beings which it enters: it is a physics of primary or bare matter. Categories of power are therefore determinations unique to the 'particular' action and its particular medium.

Discipline and Punish defines the Panopticon in this way: it is the pure function of imposing a particular taste or conduct on a multiplicity of particular individuals, provided simply that the multiplicity is small in number and the space limited and confined. No account is taken either of the forms which give the function ends and means (education, care, punishment, production) or of the formed substances acted upon by the function ('prisoners, the sick, schoolchildren, madmen, workers, soldiers', and so on). And, in fact, at the end of the eighteenth century the Panopticon traverses all these forms and is applied to all these substances: it is in this sense that a category of power exists, as a pure disciplinary function. Foucault will therefore name this the *diagram*, a function that must be 'detached from any specific use', as from any specified substance.[4]

The History of Sexuality will discuss another function which emerges at the same time: that of administering and controlling life in a particular multiplicity, provided the multiplicity is large (a population) and the space spread out or open. It is here that 'making something probable' takes on its meaning, among the categories of power, and methods of probability are introduced. In brief, the two pure functions in modern societies will be 'anatomo-politics' and 'bio-politics', and the two bare matters those of a particular body and a particular population.[5] We can therefore define the diagram in several different, interlocking ways: it is the presentation of the relations between forces unique to a particular formation; it is the distribution of the power to affect and the power to be affected; it is the mixing of non-formalized pure functions and unformed pure matter.

Between the relations between forces constituting Power and the relations between forms constituting Knowledge, is there not once again a difference similar to the one experienced between the two forms or formal elements of knowledge? Between power and knowledge there is a difference in nature or a heterogeneity; but there is also mutual presupposition and capture; and there is ultimately a primacy of the one over the other. First of all there is a difference in nature, since power does not pass through forms, but only through forces. Knowledge concerns formed matters (substances) and formalized functions, divided up segment by segment according to the two great formal conditions of seeing and speaking, light and language: it is therefore stratified, archivized, and endowed with a relatively rigid segmentarity. Power, on the other hand, is diagrammatic: it mobilizes non-stratified matter and functions, and unfolds with a very flexible segmentarity. In fact, it passes not so much through forms as through particular *points* which on each occasion mark the application of a force, the action or reaction of a force in relation to others, that is to say an affect like 'a state of power that is always local and unstable'. This leads to a fourth definition of the diagram: it is a transmission or distribution of particular features.

These power-relations, which are simultaneously local, unstable and diffuse, do not emanate from a central point or unique locus of sovereignty, but at each moment move 'from one point to another' in a field of forces, marking inflections, resistances, twists and turns, when one changes direction, or retraces one's steps. This is why they are not 'localized' at any given moment. They constitute a strategy, an exercise of the non-stratified, and these 'anonymous strategies' are almost mute and blind, since they evade all stable forms of the visible and the articulable.[6] Strategies differ from stratifications, as diagrams differ from archives. It is the instability of power-relations which defines a strategic or non-stratified environment. Power relations are therefore not *known*. Here again Foucault somewhat resembles Kant, in whom a purely practical determination is irreducible to any theoretical determination or knowledge [*connaissance*]. It is true that, in Foucault, everything is practical; but the practice of power remains irreducible to any practice of knowledge [*savoir*]. To mark this difference in nature, Foucault will say that power refers back to a 'microphysics'. But we must not take 'micro' to mean a simple miniaturization of visible and articulable forms; instead it signifies another domain, a new type of relations, a dimension of thought that is irreducible to knowledge. 'Micro' therefore means mobile and non-localizable connections.[7]

Reviewing Foucault's pragmatism, François Châtelet speaks of 'power as exercise, knowledge as regulation'.[8] The study of stratified relations of knowledge culminated in *The Archaeology of Knowledge*. The study of strategic power relations begins with *Discipline and Punish* and culminates paradoxically in *The History of Sexuality*. For the difference in nature between power and knowledge does not prevent mutual presupposition and capture, a mutual immanence. The sciences of man are inseparable from the power relations which make them possible, and provoke forms of knowledge [*savoirs*] which can more or less cross an epistemological threshold or create a practical knowledge [*connaissance*]: for example, a 'scientia sexualis' involves the relation between penitent and confessor, believer and director; while psychology involves disciplinary relations. We are not saying that the sciences of man emanate from prison, but that they presuppose the diagram of forces on which prison itself depends.

Conversely, relations between forces will remain transitive, unstable, faint, almost virtual, at all events unknown, unless they are carried out by the formed or stratified relations which make up forms of knowledge [*savoirs*]. Even the knowledge of

Nature, and above all crossing a threshold of scientificity, refer back to relations of force between men, but are themselves actualized in this form: knowledge [*connaissance*] never refers back to a subject who is free in relation to a diagram of power; but neither is the latter ever free in relation to the forces of knowledge [*savoirs*] which actualize it. This leads to the affirmation of a complex of power and knowledge that ties together the diagram and the archive, and articulates them on the basis of their difference in nature: 'Between techniques of knowledge and strategies of power, there is no exteriority, even if they have their specific roles and are linked together *on the basis of their difference.*'[9]

Power-relations are the differential relations which determine particular features (affects). The actualization which stabilizes and stratifies them is an integration: an operation which consists of tracing 'a line of general force', linking, aligning and homogenizing particular features, placing them in series and making them converge.[10] Yet there is no immediate global integration. There is, rather, a multiplicity of local and partial integrations, each one entertaining an affinity with certain relations or particular points. The integrating factors or agents of stratification make up institutions: not just the State, but also the Family, Religion, Production, the Marketplace, Art itself, Morality, and so on. The institutions are not sources or essences, and have neither essence nor interiority. They are practices or operating mechanisms which do not explain power, since they presuppose its relations and are content to 'fix' them, as part of a function that is not productive but reproductive. There is no State, only state control, and the same holds for all other cases.

This is so true that for each historical formation we must ask what belongs to each institution existing on this stratum, that is to say what power relations it integrates, what relations it entertains with other institutions, and how these divisions change from one stratum to the next. Even here these are

problems of capture that vary greatly, on both a horizontal
and a vertical level. If the State-form, in our historical formations, has captured so many power relations, this is not
because they are derived from it; on the contrary, it is because
an operation of 'continual state control', which depending on
the case in point can vary greatly, was produced in the
pedagogical, juridical, economic, familial and sexual domains
which encouraged global integration. At all events, far from
being the source of power relations, the State already implies
them. Foucault expresses this by saying that government
comes before the State, if by 'government' we understand *the
power to affect in all its aspects* (the government of children, of
souls, of the sick, of families, and so on).[11] If from then on we
try to define the most general character of the institution,
whether or not this is a State, it seems to consist of organizing
the relations which are supposed to exist between power and
government, and which are molecular or 'microphysical' relations, around a molar agency: 'the' Sovereign or 'the' Law, in
the case of the State; the Father in the case of the family;
Money, Gold or the Dollar in the case of the market; God in
the case of religion; Sex in the case of the sexual institution.
The History of Sexuality will analyse these two privileged examples, Law and Sex, and the book's whole conclusion shows
how the differential relations of a 'sexuality without sex' are
integrated into the speculative element of sex as being 'a
unique signifier and a universal signified', which normalizes
desire by 'hystericizing' sexuality. But always, rather as in
Proust, a molecular sexuality bubbles away beneath the
surface of the integrated sexes.

It is these integrations or molar agencies which constitute
forms of knowledge [*savoirs*] (for example, a 'scientia
sexualis'). But why does a fissure appear at this level?
Foucault remarks that an institution necessarily has two poles
or elements: 'apparatuses' and 'rules'. In fact it organizes
great visibilities, fields of visibility, and great articulable
elements, systems of statements. The institution has two forms

or faces (sex, for example, is the sex that both speaks and reveals, language and light).[12] More generally, we again obtain the result of previous analyses: integration actualizes or operates only by also creating *divergent* ways of actualizing, and by dividing itself up among them. Or rather, actualization integrates only by also creating *a system of formal differentiation*. In each formation there is a form of receptivity that constitutes the visible element, and a form of spontaneity that constitutes the articulable element. Of course, these two forms do not coincide with the two aspects of force or the two sorts of affects, the receptivity of power's ability to be affected and the spontaneity of power's ability to affect. But the two forms are derived from these affects, and find in them their 'internal conditions'. For the power relation has no form in itself, but establishes contact between unformed matter (receptivity) and unformalized functions (spontaneity). On the other hand relations of knowledge, on each side, deal with formed substances and formalized functions by using the receptive kind of visible element, or the spontaneous kind of articulable element.

Formed substances are revealed by visibility, while formalized or finalized functions are revealed by statement. There is no confusion, therefore, between the affective categories of power (of the 'incite' and 'provoke' variety) and the formal categories of knowledge (such as 'educate', 'look after', 'punish', and so on), the latter passing through seeing and speaking in order to actualize the former. But it is precisely for this reason, by virtue of this displacement which excludes coincidence, that the institution has the capacity to integrate power-relations, by constituting various forms of knowledge which actualize, modify and *redistribute* these relations. And depending on the nature of the institution in question, or rather depending on how it operates, visibilities on the one hand and statements on the other will attain a certain threshold that will make them political, economic, aesthetic, and so on. (One 'problem' will obviously be to know if a statement can attain a threshold, such as a scientific one, while visibility remains at a lower level. Or vice versa. But that is what makes truth a problem. There are visibilities of State, art, and sciences, as much as of statements, and they always vary).

How does this integration and actualization come about? We can at least understand one half of it, thanks to *The Archaeology of Knowledge*. There Foucault invokes 'regularity' as a property of the statement. For Foucault, regularity has a precise meaning: it is the curve joining individual points (a rule). To be precise, the relations between forces determine individual points, such that a diagram is always a transmission of particular features. But the curve which connects them by passing near them is completely different. Albert Lautman showed that there are 'two completely different realities' in mathematics, in the theory of differential equations, although they are necessarily complementary: the one is the existence and distribution of individual points in a field of vectors; the other is the form of the integral curves in their neighbourhood.[13]

This leads to a method invoked by *The Archaeology of Knowledge*: a series continues until it passes into the neighbourhood of another individual point, at which moment another series begins, which can either converge with the first one (statements from the same 'family') or else diverge (another family). It is in this sense that a curve carries out the relations of force by regularizing and aligning them, making the series converge, and tracing a 'general line of force': for Foucault, not only are curves and graphs statements, but statements are kinds of curves or graphs. To illustrate vividly this point that statements cannot be reduced either to phrases or to propositions, he says that the letters which I write at random on a sheet of paper form a statement, 'the statement of an alphabetical series governed by no other laws than those of chance';[14] in the same way the letters which I copy down from the keyboard of a French typewriter form a statement, A,

Z, E, R, T (although the keyboard and the letters to be found there are not themselves statements, since they are visibilities). On that point, if we are to bring together the most difficult or mysterious of Foucault's texts, he adds that a statement necessarily has a specific link with something outside it, with 'something which can be strangely like it and virtually identical to it'.

Must we understand from this that statements are linked to visibilities, like the letters on the keyboard? Certainly not, since it is precisely this link between the visible and the articulable elements that is in question. The statement is not at all defined by what it designates or signifies. It seems to us that what we must understand is this: *a statement is the curve joining individual points*: that is, the thing that brings about or actualizes relations between forces, such as they exist in French between the letters and the figures, depending on the degree of frequency and proximity (or, in the other example, depending on chance). But *the individual points themselves*, with their relations between forces, did not already constitute a statement: they were the outside of the statement, which the statement may strongly resemble to the point of being virtually identical.[15] As for visibilities, for example the letters on the keyboard, they are external to the statement but do not constitute its outside. From this moment on, visibilities find themselves in the same situation as statements, a statement peculiar to them which they must resolve in their own way. Visibilities must also be connected to the outside which they actualize, together with the particular features or relations between forces which in turn they integrate, but they do so in a different way and in a different mode from that of statements, since they are external to the latter.

The statement-curve integrates into language the intensity of the affects, the differential relations between forces, the particular features of power (potentialities). But visibilities must then also integrate these in a completely different way, into light. This is so much so that light, as a receptive form of integration, must follow a comparable but non-corresponding path to that of language as a form of spontaneity. And the relation between the two forms at the heart of their 'non-relation' will be the two ways in which they fix the unstable relations between forces, localize and globalize diffusions, and regularize particular points. For visibilities, in the light of historical formations, form scenes which are to the visible element what a statement is to the sayable or readable. The 'scene' has always haunted Foucault, and he often uses the word in a general manner that also covers statements. But in this way he confers on statements a general descriptive importance which does not belong precisely to them. In the most exact sense, the description-scene and the statement-curve are the two heterogeneous forces of formalization and integration.

Foucault enters into a logical tradition that is already well established, one which claims that there is a difference in nature between statements and descriptions (for example, Russell). Originating in logic, this problem has seen unexpected developments in the novel, the 'new novel' and then in the cinema. For this reason the new solution proposed by Foucault holds all the more: the description-scene is the regulation unique to visibilities, just as the statement-curve is the regulation unique to readabilities. This leads to Foucault's passion for describing scenes, or, even more so, for offering descriptions that stand as scenes: descriptions of *Las Meninas*, Manet, Magritte, the admirable descriptions of the chain gang, the asylum, the prison and the little prison van, as though they were scenes and Foucault were a painter. No doubt this is due to his affinity, to be found throughout all his work, with the new novel and with Raymond Roussel.

Let us return to the description of *Las Meninas* by Velásquez: the path of light forms a 'spiral shell' that makes the particular features visible and turns them into a series of flashes and reflections of light within a complete 'cycle' of representation.[16] Just as statements are curves before they are phrases and propositions, so scenes are lines of light before they become contours and colours. And what the scene brings about in this poem of receptivity are the particular features of a relation between forces, which in this case is the relation between the painter and the sovereign such that they 'alternate, in a never-ending flicker'. The diagram of forces is realized both in description-scenes and statement-curves.

This triangle in Foucault's work holds as much for epistemological as for aesthetic analysis. Even more, just as visibilities entail statements of capture, so statements themselves include visibilities of capture, which continue to distinguish themselves from the former even when they are operating with words. It is in this sense that a strictly literary analysis, even at its very heart, is likely to rediscover the difference between scenes and curves: descriptions may be verbal, but they are none the less different from statements. Here we are thinking of an *œuvre* like Faulkner's: statements trace fantastic curves which pass through discursive objects and mobile subject-positions (the one name for several persons, two names for the one person) and which are inscribed within a language-being, in a reunion of all the language unique to Faulkner. But the descriptions conjure up a host of scenes which create reflections, flashes, shimmerings, visibilities varying according to the time and the season, which distribute the descriptions in a light-being, a reunion of all the light to which Faulkner holds the secret (Faulkner, literature's greatest 'luminist'). And above these two elements there exists the third phenomenon, centres of power that are unknown, unseen and unsaid, the eroding or eroded focuses that are overturned and degenerate in the family from the Deep South: a whole becoming-dark.

In what sense is there primacy of power over knowledge, and of power-relations over relations of knowledge? The answer is that the latter would have nothing to integrate if there were no differential power relations. It is true that the former would fade and remain embryonic or virtual without the operations

that integrate them; this is what leads to mutual presupposition. But if there is primacy it is because the two
heterogeneous forms of knowledge are constituted by integration and enter into an indirect relation, above and beyond
their interstice or their 'non-relation', under conditions
pertaining only to the forces. In this way the indirect relation
between the two forms of knowledge does not imply any
common form, or even a correspondence, but only the informal
element of forces in which both are steeped. Foucault's
diagrammaticism, that is to say the presentation of pure relations between forces or the transmission of pure particular
features, is therefore the analogue of Kantian schematicism: it
is this that ensures the relation from which knowledge flows,
between the two irreducible forms of spontaneity and receptivity. And this holds in so far as the force itself enjoys a
spontaneity and receptivity which are unique to it even though
they are informal, or rather because they are informal. No
doubt power, if we consider it in the abstract, neither sees nor
speaks. It is a mole that only knows its way round its network of
tunnels, its multiple hole: it 'acts on the basis of innumerable
points'; it 'comes from below'. But precisely because it does not
itself speak and see, it makes us see and speak.

How can we present Foucault's project on 'the life of infamous men'? It does not deal with famous men who already
had both words and light at their disposal and became famous
for their evil. It deals instead with criminal existences which are
dark and mute and are momentarily dragged out into the light
and made to speak by their encounter or clash with power. We
can even say that if no original, free and savage experience lies
beneath knowledge, as phenomenology would have it, it is
because Seeing and Speaking are always already completely
caught up within power relations which they presuppose and
actualize.[17] For example, if we try to establish a body of phrases
and texts in order to isolate its statements, we succeed only if we
designate the centres of power (and resistance) on which this
body depends.

This is the essential point: if power relations imply relations of knowledge, the latter also presuppose the former. If statements exist only as something dispersed within a form of exteriority, and if visibilities exist only as something disseminated within another form of exteriority, this is because power relations are themselves diffuse, multipunctual, lying within an element that no longer even has any form. Power relations designate 'the other thing' to which statements (and also visibilities) refer, even if these latter elements are virtually indistinguishable, due to the imperceptible and continuous operation of the integrators: as *The Archaeology of Knowledge* states, the random transmission of numbers is not a statement, but their vocal or written reproduction *is*. If power is not simply violence, this is not only because it passes in itself through categories that express the relation between two forces (inciting, inducing, producing a useful effect, etc.) but also because, in relation to knowledge, it produces truth, in so far as it makes us see and speak.[18] It produces truth as a problem.

The above study presented us with a dualism peculiar to Foucault, existing on the level of knowledge, between the visual and the articulable. But we must note that in general a dualism has at least three meanings: it involves a real dualism marking an irreducible difference between two substances, as in Descartes, or between two faculties, as in Kant; or it involves a provisional stage that subsequently becomes a monism, as in Spinoza or Bergson; or else it involves a pre-liminary distribution operating at the heart of a pluralism. Foucault represents this last case. For if the visible and the articulable elements enter into a duel, it is to the extent that their respective forms, as forms of exteriority, dispersion or dissemination, make up two types of 'multiplicity', neither of which can be reduced to a unity: statements exist only in a discursive multiplicity, and visibilities in a non-discursive multiplicity. And these two multiplicities open up on to a third: a multiplicity of relations between forces, a multiplicity of diffusion which no longer splits into two and is free of any dualizable form.

Discipline and Punish continually demonstrates that dualisms are molar or massive effects occurring within 'multiplicities'. And the dualism of force, the ability to affect and be affected, is merely the index in each one of the multiplicity of forces, the multiple being of force. Syberberg once said that dividing something into two is an attempt to distribute a multiplicity which cannot be represented by a single form.[19] But this distribution can only distinguish multiplicities from multiplicities. This is the whole of Foucault's philosophy, which is a pragmatics of the multiple.

If the variable combinations of the two forms, the visible and the articulable, constitute strata or historical formations, the microphysics of power, on the contrary, exposes the relations between forces in an informal and non-stratified element. In this way the supersensitive diagram does not merge with the audiovisual archive: it is like the *a priori* element presupposed by the historical formation. However, there is nothing lying beneath, above, or even outside the strata. The relations between forces, which are mobile, faint and diffuse, do not lie outside strata but form the outside of strata. This is why the elements *a priori* to history are themselves historical. We might at first glance think that the diagram is reserved for modern societies: *Discipline and Punish* analyses the disciplinary diagram in so far as it replaces the effects of the old sovereign regime with a control that is immanent to the social field. But this is not at all the case; it is each stratified historical formation which refers back to a diagram of forces as though it were its outside.

Our disciplinary societies are channelled through categories of power (actions upon actions) that we can define as imposing some kind of task or producing a useful effect, controlling a population or administering life. But the old sovereign societies were defined by other categories that were no less diagrammatic: levying (the action of levying on actions or products, the force of levying on forces) and bestowing life or death ('to take life or let live', which is very different from administering life).[20] In both cases there is a diagram. Foucault also indicated another diagram referred to by the Church community rather than State society, a 'pastoral' diagram whose categories he gave as grazing a flock, and so on, a relation between forces or an action upon an action.[21] We can speak of a Greek diagram, as we shall see; of a Roman diagram, of a feudal diagram, and so on. The list is endless, like that of the categories of power (and the disciplinary diagram is certainly not the last word on the subject).

In a way we could say that the diagrams communicate, above, below or between the respective strata (it is in this way that we can define a 'Napoleonic' diagram as being an inter-stratic, intermediary stage between the old sovereign society and the new disciplinary society which it prefigures).[22] And it is indeed in this sense that the diagram differs from strata: only the stratified formation gives it a stability that it does not itself possess, for in itself it is unstable, agitated and shuffled around. This is the paradoxical character of the *a priori* element, a microagitation. For the forces in the relation are inseparable from the variations in their relations or their distances from one another. In brief, forces are in a perpetual state of evolution; *there is an emergence of forces which doubles history*, or rather envelopes it, according to the Nietzschean conception. This means that the diagram, in so far as it exposes a set of relations between forces, is not a place but rather 'a non-place': it is the place only of mutation. Suddenly, things are no longer perceived or propositions articulated in the same way.[23]

No doubt the diagram communicates with the stratified formation stabilizing or fixing it, but following another axis it also communicates with the other diagram, the other unstable diagrammatic states, through which forces pursue their mutant emergence. This is why the diagram always represents the outside of the strata. There is no display of the relations between forces that is not simultaneously a transmission of particular points or features. Not that anything can be linked up with anything else. Instead it is more like a series of draws in a lottery, each one operating at random but under extrinsic conditions laid down by the previous draw. The diagram or diagram state is always a mixture of the aleatory and the dependent, like a Markov chain.* Foucault quotes Nietzsche's remark about 'the iron hand of necessity throwing the dice of chance'. Things are not joined together by a process of continuity or interiorization, therefore, but instead they rejoin above and beyond the breaks and discontinuities (mutation).

We must distinguish between exteriority and the outside. Exteriority is still a form, as in *The Archaeology of Knowledge* – even two forms which are exterior to one another, since knowledge is made from the two environments of light and language, seeing and speaking. But the outside concerns force: if force is always in relation with other forces, forces necessarily refer to an irreducible outside which no longer even has any form and is made up of distances that cannot be broken down through which one force acts upon another or is acted upon by another. It is always from the outside that a force confers on others or receives from others the variable position to be found only at a particular distance or in a particular relation. There is therefore an emergence of forces which remains distinct from the history of forms, since it operates in a different dimension. It is *an outside which is farther away* than any external world and even any form of exteriority, which henceforth becomes infintely closer.

And how could the two forms of exteriority be external to one another, if there were not this outside, which is both closer and farther away? This is 'the other thing', already mentioned by *The Archaeology of Knowledge*. And if the two formal elements of knowledge, external and heterogeneous, find historical accords which provide solutions for the 'problem' of truth, this

---

*(in statistics) A sequence of events; the probability of each is dependent only on the event immediately preceding.

is, as we have seen, because forces operate in a different space to that of forms, the space of the Outside, where the relation is precisely a 'non-relation', the place a 'non-place', and history an emergence.

In Foucault's work the article on Nietzsche and the one on Blanchot join up, or rejoin. If seeing and speaking are forms of exteriority, thinking addresses itself to an outside that has no form.[24] To think is to reach the non-stratified. Seeing is thinking, and speaking is thinking, but thinking occurs in the interstice, or the disjunction between seeing and speaking. This is Foucault's second point of contact with Blanchot: thinking belongs to the outside in so far as the latter, an 'abstract storm', is swallowed up by the interstice between seeing and speaking. The appeal to the outside is a constant theme in Foucault and signifies that thinking is not the innate exercise of a faculty, but must become thought. Thinking does not depend on a beautiful interiority that would reunite the visible and the articulable elements, but is carried under the intrusion of an outside that eats into the interval and forces or dismembers the internal. 'When the outside collapses and attracts interiority', the interior presupposes a beginning and an end, an origin and a destination that can coincide and incorporate 'everything'. But when there are only environments and whatever lies between them, when words and things are opened up by the environment without ever coinciding, there is a liberation of forces which come from the outside and exist only in a mixed-up state of agitation, modification and mutation. In truth, they are dice-throws, for thinking involves throwing the dice.

This is what we are told by the forces of the outside: the transformation occurs not to the historical, stratified and archaeological composition but to the composing forces, when the latter enter into a relation with other forces which have come from outside (strategies). Emergence, change and mutation affect composing forces, not composed forms. Why is this idea, apparently so simple, difficult to understand to the point where the 'death of man' has caused so much misinterpretation? Either the objection was raised that it was not a question of real men but only a concept of man; or else it was felt that Foucault and Nietzsche saw real man transcending himself and, they hoped, becoming a superman. In both cases, we have a total misinterpretation of Foucault as well as Nietzsche (we shall leave aside the question of the malevolence and stupidity to be found sometimes in commentaries on Foucault, as was the case with Nietzsche).

In fact the question is not that of the human compound, whether conceptual or real, perceptible or articulable. The question concerns the forces that make up man: with what other forces do they combine, and what is the compound that emerges? In the classical age all the forces of man are referred back to a force of 'representation' that claims to isolate the positive elements, those that *can be raised to infinity*, such that the set of forces makes up God and not man, while man can emerge only between categories of infinity. This is why Merleau-Ponty defined classical thought by the innocent way in which it conceived of infinity: not only did infinity predate finity, but the qualities of man, once raised to infinity, served to make up the unfathomable unity of God. In order for man to appear as a specific compound, the forces that create him enter into a relation with new forces which evade that of representation, even to the point of deposing it. These new forces are those of life, work and language, in so far as life discovers an 'organization', work a 'production', and language a 'filiation', qualities which put them outside representation. *These dark forces of finitude are not initially human* but enter into a relation with the forces of man in order to bring him down to his own finitude, and communicate to him a history which he then proceeds to make his own.[25]

In this new historical formation of the nineteenth century, it is indeed man who is made up from the set of composing forces 'drawn' from the lottery. But if we can imagine a third draw, the forces of man will enter into a relation with other forces again in such a way as to make up something else that will no longer be either God or man: we could say that the death of man links up with that of God, to create new compounds. In brief, the relation between composing forces and the outside continually changes the compound form, in other relations, as it is taken up and transformed by new compositions. We must take quite literally the idea that man is a face drawn in the sand between two tides: he is a composition appearing only between two others, a classical past that never knew him, and a future that will no longer know him.[26] There is no occasion either for rejoicing or for weeping. Is it not commonplace nowadays to say that the forces of man have already entered into a relation with the forces of information technology and their third-generation machines which together create something other than man, indivisible 'man-machine' systems? Is this a union with silicon instead of carbon?

It is still from the outside that a force affects, or is affected by, others. The power to affect or be affected is carried out in a variable way, depending on the forces involved in the relation. The diagram, as the fixed form of a set of relations between forces, never exhausts force, which can enter into other relations and compositions. The diagram stems from the outside but the outside does not merge with any diagram, and continues instead to 'draw' new ones. In this way the outside is always an opening on to a future: nothing ends, since nothing has begun, but everything is transformed. In this sense force displays potentiality with respect to the diagram containing it, or possesses a third power which presents itself as the possibility of 'resistance'. In fact, alongside (or rather opposite) particular features of power which correspond to its relations, a diagram of forces presents particular features of resistance, such as 'points, knots or focuses' which act in turn on the strata, but in such a way as to make change possible.[27] Moreover, the final word on power is that *resistance comes first*, to the extent that power relations operate completely within the diagram, while resistances necessarily operate in a direct relation with the outside from which the diagrams emerge.[28]

This means that a social field offers more resistance than strategies, and the thought of the outside is a thought of resistance.

Three centuries ago certain fools were astonished because Spinoza wished to see the liberation of man, even though he did not believe in his liberty or even in his particular existence. Today new fools, or even the same ones reincarnated, are astonished because the Foucault who had spoken of the death of man took part in political struggle. In opposition to Foucault, they invoke a universal and eternal consciousness of the rights of man which must not be subjected to analysis. This is not the first time an idea has been called eternal in order to mask the fact that it is actually weak or summary and is not even aware of those elements that might sustain it (such as the changes that have taken place in modern law since the nineteenth century).

It is true that Foucault has never accorded great importance to universal or eternal questions: they are merely massive or global effects arising out of a certain distribution of particular features, in a particular historical formation and a particular process of formalization. Beneath the universal there are games or transmissions of particular features, and the universal or eternal nature of man is merely the shadow of a particular and ephemeral combination carried by a historical stratum. The only case in which the universal is stated at the same time as the statement appears is in mathematics, because the 'threshold of formalization' coincides with the threshold of apparition. But anywhere else, the universal comes after.[29]

Foucault can 'denounce the movement of a logos which raises the particular elements to the status of a concept', because 'this logos is in fact only an already established discourse' that remains when everything has been said, when everything is already dead and has returned to 'the silent interiority of self-consciousness'.[30] The subject of law, in so far as it is made, is life, which is the bearer of particular elements, 'a plenitude of the possible'; not man, who is the form of eternity. And of course man replaced life, and the subject of law, when for a moment his image was composed of vital forces during the political era of Constitutions. But today law has again changed subject because, even *within men*, the vital forces are entering into new combinations and composing new figures:

> What was understood and what served as an objective was life . . . It was life far more than the law which became the issue of political struggles, even if the latter were formulated through affirmations concerning rights. The 'right' to life, to one's body, to health, to happiness, to the satisfaction of needs . . . this 'right' which the classical juridical system was utterly incapable of comprehending.[31]

It is this same change that we are observing in the status of 'the intellectual'. In the course of several published interviews, Foucault explains that the individual could lay claim to universality during a long period stretching from the eighteenth century right up to the Second World War (perhaps up to Sartre, by way of Zola, Rolland, and so on): this was to the extent that the uniqueness of the writer coincided with the position of a 'jurist' or 'notable' who could hold out against the professionals in law, and so produce an effect of universality. If the intellectual has changed face (as well as the function of writing), it is because his very position has changed and he now tends to move from one specific place or point to another, that of the 'atomic physicist or geneticist or information technologist or pharmacologist, and so on', in this way producing effects not of universality but of transversality, and functioning as an exchanger or privileged junction.[32] In this way the intellectual or even the writer can (at least potentially) participate all the more in current struggles and resistance, now that these have become 'transversal'. So the intellectual or the writer becomes adept at speaking the language of life, rather than of law.

What is Foucault trying to say in the best pages of *The History of Sexuality*? When the diagram of power abandons the model of sovereignty in favour of a disciplinary model, when it becomes the 'bio-power' or 'bio-politics' of populations, controlling and administering life, it is indeed life that emerges as the new object of power. At that point law increasingly renounces that symbol of sovereign privilege, the right to put someone to death (the death penalty), but allows itself to produce all the more hecatombs and genocides: not by returning to the old law of killing, but on the contrary in the name of race, precious space, conditions of life and the survival of a population that believes itself to be better than its enemy, which it now treats not as the juridical enemy of the old sovereign but as a toxic or infectious agent, a sort of 'biological danger'. From that point on the death penalty tends to be abolished and holocausts grow 'for the same reasons', testifying all the more effectively to the death of man. But when power in this way takes life as its aim or object, then resistance to power already puts itself on the side of life, and turns life against power: 'life as a political object was in a sense taken at face value and turned back against the system that was bent on controlling it'.

Contrary to a fully established discourse, there is no need to uphold man in order to resist. What resistance extracts from this revered old man, as Nietzsche put it, is the forces of a life that is larger, more active, more affirmative and richer in possibilities. The superman has never meant anything but that: it is in man himself that we must liberate life, since man himself is a form of imprisonment for man. Life becomes resitance to power when power takes life as its object. Here again, the two operations belong to the same horizon (we can see this clearly in the question of abortion, when the most reactionary powers invoke a 'right to live'). When power becomes bio-power resistance becomes the power of life, a vital power that cannot be confined within species, environment or the paths of a particular diagram. Is not the force that comes from outside a certain idea of Life, a certain vitalism, in which Foucault's thought culminates? Is not life this capacity to resist force? From *The Birth of the Clinic* on, Foucault admired Bichat for having invented a new vitalism by defining life as the set of those functions which resist death.[33] And for Foucault as much as for Nietzsche, it is in man himself that we must look for the set of forces and functions which resist the death of man. Spinoza said that there was no telling what the human body might achieve, once freed from human discipline. To which Foucault replies that there is no telling what man might achieve 'as a living being', as the set of forces that resist.[34]

Foldings, or the Inside of Thought (Subjectivation)

What happened during the fairly long silence following *The History of Sexuality*? Perhaps Foucault felt slightly uneasy about the book: had he not trapped himself within the concept of power relations? He himself put forward the following objection: 'That's just like you, always with the same *incapacity to cross the line*, to pass over to the other side . . . it is always the same choice, for the side of power, for what power says or of what it causes to be said.'[1] And no doubt his own reply was that 'the most intense point of lives, the one where their energy is concentrated, is precisely where they clash with power, struggle with it, endeavour to utilize its forces or to escape its traps.' He might equally have added that the diffuse centres of power do not exist without points of resistance that are in some way primary; and that power does not take life as its objective without revealing or giving rise to a life that resists power; and finally that the force of the outside continues to disrupt the diagrams and turn them upside down.

But what happens, on the other hand, if the transversal relations of resistance continue to become restratified, and to encounter or even construct knots of power? Already the ultimate failure of the prison movement, after 1970, had saddened Foucault, on top of which other events, on a world scale, must have saddened him even more. If power is constitutive of truth, how can we conceive of a 'power of truth' which would no longer be the truth of power, a truth that would release transversal lines of resistance and not integral lines of power? How can we 'cross the line'? And, if we must attain a life that is the power of the outside, what tells us that this outside is not a terrifying void and that this life, which seems to put up a resistance, is not just the simple distribution within the void of 'slow, partial and progressive' deaths? We can no longer even say that death transforms life into destiny, an 'indivisible and decisive' event, but rather that death becomes multiplied and differentiated in order to bestow on life the particular features, and consequently the truths, which life believes arise from resisting death. What remains, then, if not to pass through all these deaths preceding the great limit of death itself, deaths which even afterwards continue? Life henceforth consists only of taking one's place, or every place, in the cortège of a 'One dies'.

It is in this sense that Bichat broke with the classical conception of death, as a decisive moment or indivisible event, and broke with it in two ways, simultaneously presenting death as being coextensive with life and as something made up of a multiplicity of partial and particular deaths. When Foucault analyses Bichat's theories, his tone demonstrates sufficiently that he is concerned with something other than an epistemological analysis[2]: he is concerned with a conception of death, and few men more than Foucault died in a way commensurate with their conception of death. This force of life that belonged to Foucault was always thought through and lived out as a multiple death in the manner of Bichat.

What remains, then, except an anonymous life that shows up only when it clashes with power, argues with it, exchanges 'brief and strident words', and then fades back into the night, what Foucault called 'the life of infamous men', whom he asked us to admire by virtue of 'their misfortune, rage or uncertain madness'?[3] Strangely, implausibly, it is this 'infamy' which he claimed for himself: 'My point of departure was those sorts of particles endowed with an energy that is all the greater for their being small and difficult to spot.' This culminated in *The Use of Pleasure*'s searing phrase: 'to get free of oneself'.[4]

The History of Sexuality explicitly closes on a doubt. If at the end of it Foucault finds himself in an impasse, this is not because of his conception of power but rather because he found the impasse to be where power itself places us, in both our lives and our thoughts, as we run up against it in our smallest truths. This could be resolved only if the outside were caught up in a movement that would snatch it away from the void and pull it back from death. This would be like a new axis, different from the axes of both knowledge and power. Could this axis be the place where a sense of serenity would be finally attained and life truly affirmed? In any case, it is not an axis that annuls all others but one that was already working at the same time as the others, and prevented them from closing on the impassse. Perhaps this third axis was present from the beginning in Foucault (just as power was present from the beginning in knowledge). But it could emerge only by assuming a certain distance, and so being able to circle back on the other two. Foucault felt it necessary to carry out a general reshuffle in order to unravel this path which was so tangled up in the others that it remained hidden: it is this recentring which Foucault puts forward in the general introduction to *The Use of Pleasure*.

But how was this new dimension present from the beginning? Up until now, we have encountered three dimensions: the relations which have been formed or formalized along certain strata (Knowledge); the relations between forces to be found at the level of the diagram (Power); and the relation with the outside, that absolute relation, as Blanchot says, which is also a non-relation (Thought). Does this mean that there is no inside? Foucault continually submits interiority to a radical critique. But is there *an inside that lies deeper than any internal world*, just as the outside is farther away than any external world? The outside is not a fixed limit but a moving matter animated by peristaltic movements, folds and foldings that together make up an inside: they are not something other than the outside, but precisely the inside *of* the outside. *The Order of Things* developed this theme: if thought comes from outside, and remains attached to the outside, how come the outside does not flood into the inside, as the element that thought does not and cannot think of? The unthought is therefore not external to thought but lies at its very heart, as that impossibility of thinking which doubles or hollows out the outside.[5]

The classical age had already stated that there was an inside of thought, the unthought, when it invoked the finite, the different orders of infinity. And from the nineteenth century on it is more the dimensions of finitude which fold the outside and constitute a 'depth', a 'density withdrawn into itself', an inside to life, labour and language, in which man is embedded, if only to sleep, but conversely which is also itself embedded in man 'as a living being, a working individual or a speaking subject'.[6] Either it is the fold of the infinite, or the constant folds [*replis*] of finitude which curve the outside and constitute the inside. *The Birth of the Clinic* had already shown how the clinic brought the body up to the surface, but equally how pathological anatomy subsequently introduced into this body deep foldings which did not resuscitate the old notion of interiority but constituted instead the new inside of this outside.[7]

The inside as an operation of the outside: in all his work Foucault seems haunted by this theme of an inside which is merely the fold of the outside, as if the ship were a folding of the sea. On the subject of the Renaissance madman who is put to sea in his boat, Foucault wrote:

> he is put in the interior of the exterior, and inversely [. . .] a prisoner in the midst of what is the freest, the openest of routes: bound fast at the infinite crossroads. He is the Passenger *par excellence*: that is, the prisoner of the passage.[8]

Thought has no other being than this madman himself. As Blanchot says of Foucault: 'He encloses the outside, that is, constitutes it in an interiority of expectation or exception.'[9]

Or, rather, the theme which has always haunted Foucault is

that of the double. But the double is never a projection of the interior; on the contrary, it is an interiorization of the outside. It is not a doubling of the One, but a redoubling of the Other. It is not a reproduction of the Same, but a repetition of the Different. It is not the emanation of an 'I', but something that places in immanence an always other or a Non-self. It is never the other who is a double in the doubling process, it is a self that lives me as the double of the other: I do not encounter myself on the outside, I find the other in me ('it is always concerned with showing how the Other, the Distant, is also the Near and the Same').[10] It resembles exactly the invagination of a tissue in embryology, or the act of doubling in sewing: twist, fold, stop, and so on.

The Archaeology of Knowledge showed, in its most paradoxical pages, how one phrase was the repetition of another, and above all how one statement repeated or doubled 'something else' that was barely distinguishable from it (the transmission of letters on the keyboard, AZERT). Equally, the books on power showed how the stratified forms repeated relations between forces that were barely distinguishable from one another, and how history was the doubling of an emergence. This permanent theme in Foucault had already been analysed in depth in *Raymond Roussel*. For what Raymond Roussel had discovered was the phrase of the outside, its repetition in a second phrase, the minuscule difference between the two (the 'snag' [*l'accroc*]) and the twisting and doubling from one to the other. The snag is no longer the accident of the tissue but the new rule on the basis of which the external tissue is twisted, invaginated and doubled. The 'facultative' rule, or the transmission of chance, a dice-throw. They are, says Foucault, games of repetition, of difference, and of the doubling that 'links them'.

This is not the only time Foucault presents in a literary and humorous way what could be demonstrated by epistemology or linguistics, which are both serious disciplines. *Raymond Roussel* has knitted or sewn together all the meanings of the word *doublure*, in order to show how the inside was always the folding of a presupposed outside.[11] And Roussel's last method, the proliferation of parentheses inside one another, multiplies the foldings within the sentence. This is why Foucault's book on Roussel is important, and no doubt the path it traces is itself double. This does not at all mean that the primacy can be reversed: the inside will always be the doubling *of* the outside. But it does mean that either, like Roussel recklessly searching for death, we want to undo the doubling and pull away the folds 'with a studied gesture', in order to reach the outside and its 'stifling hollowness'; or like Leiris, who is more wise and prudent but none the less in another sense incredibly audacious, we follow the folds, reinforce the doublings from snag to snag, and surround ourselves with foldings that form an 'absolute memory', in order to make the outside into a vital, recurring element.[12] As *The History of Madness* put it: to be put in the interior of the exterior, and inversely. Perhaps Foucault has always oscillated between the two forms of the double, already characterized at this early stage as the choice between death or memory. Perhaps he chose death, like Roussel, but not without having passed through the detours or foldings of memory.

Perhaps he even had to go back to the Greeks. In this way even the most impassioned problem would be given a context that would restore a sense of calm. If folding or doubling haunts all Foucault's work, but surfaces only at a late stage, this is because he gave the name of 'absolute memory' to a new dimension which had to be distinguished both from relations between forces or power-relations and from stratified forms of knowledge. Greek education presents new power-relations which are very different from the old imperial forms of education and materialize in a Greek light as a system of visibility, and in a Greek logos as a system of statements. We can therefore speak of a diagram of power which extends across all qualified forms of knowledge: 'governing oneself, managing one's estate, and participating in the administration of the city were three practices of the same type', and Xenophon 'shows the continuity and isomorphism between the three "arts", as well as the chronological sequence by which they were to be practised in the life of an individual.'[13] However, not even this marks the great novelty of the Greeks. Such novelty ultimately emerges thanks to a double unhooking or 'differentiation' [*décrochage*]: when the 'exercises that enabled one to govern oneself' *become detached* both from power as a relation between forces, and from knowledge as a stratified form, or 'code' of virtue. On the one hand there is a 'relation to oneself' that consciously derives from one's relation with others; on the other there is equally a 'self-constitution' that consciously derives from the moral code as a rule for knowledge.[14]

This derivative or differentiation must be understood in the sense in which the *relation to oneself* assumes an independent status. It is as if the relations of the outside folded back to create a doubling, allow a relation to oneself to emerge, and constitute an inside which is hollowed out and develops its own unique dimension: 'enkrateia', the relation to oneself that is self-mastery, 'is a power that one brought to bear on oneself *in* the power that one exercised over others' (how could one claim to govern others if one could not govern oneself?) to the point where the relation to oneself becomes 'a principle of internal regulation' in relation to the constituent powers of politics, the family, eloquence, games and even virtue.[15] This is the Greek version of the snag and the doubling: a differentiation that leads to a folding, a reflection.

This, at least, is Foucault's version of the novelty of the Greeks. And this version appears very important in both its detail and its superficial modesty. What the Greeks did is not to reveal Being or unfold the Open in a world-historical gesture. According to Foucault they did a great deal less, or more.[16] They bent the outside, through a series of practical exercises. The Greeks are the first doubling. Force is what belongs to the outside, since it is essentially a relation between other forces: it is inseparable in itself from the power to affect other forces (spontaneity) and to be affected by others (receptivity). But what comes about as a result is *a relation which force has with itself, a power to affect itself, an affect of self on self.* Following the Greek diagram, only free men can dominate others ('free agents' and the 'agonistic relations' between them are diagrammatic characteristics).[17] But how could they dominate others if they could not dominate themselves? The domination of others must be doubled by a domination of oneself. The relation with others must be doubled by a relation with oneself. The obligatory rules for power must be doubled by facultative rules for the free man who exercises power. As moral codes here and there execute the diagram (in the city, the family, tribunals, games, etc.), a 'subject' must be isolated which differentiates itself from the code and no longer has an internal dependence on it.

This is what the Greeks did: they folded force, even though it still remained force. They made it relate back to itself. Far from ignoring interiority, individuality or subjectivity they invented the subject, but only as a derivative or the product of a 'subjectivation': They discovered the 'aesthetic existence' – the doubling or relation with oneself, the facultative rule of free man.[18] (If we do not regard this derivation as being a new dimension, then we must say that there is no sense of subjectivity in the Greeks, especially if we look for it on the level of obligatory rules.) Foucault's fundamental idea is that of a dimension of subjectivity derived from power and knowledge without being dependent on them.

In another way it is *The Use of Pleasure* which in several respects differentiates from the previous books. On the one hand it invokes a long period of time that begins with the Greeks and continues up to the present day by way of Christianity, while the previous books considered short periods, between the seventeenth and nineteenth centuries. On the other it discovers the relation to oneself, as a new dimension that cannot be reduced to the power-relations and relations between forms of knowledge that were the object of previous books: the whole system has to be reorganized. Finally, there is a break with *The History of Sexuality*, which studied sexuality from the double viewpoint of power and knowledge; now the relation to oneself is laid bare, but its links with sexuality remain uncertain.[20] Consequently, the first step in a complete reorganization is already there: does the relation to oneself have an elective affinity with sexuality, to the point of renewing the project of a 'history of sexuality'?

The reply is a vigorous one: just as power-relations can be affirmed only by being carried out, so the relation to oneself, which bends these power relations, can be established only by being carried out. And it is in sexuality that it is established or carried out. Perhaps not immediately; for the constitution of an inside or interiority is alimentary before it is sexual.[21] But here again, what is it that leads sexuality to 'differentiate' itself gradually from alimentary considerations and become the place in which the relation to oneself is enacted? The reason is that sexuality, as it is lived out by the Greeks, incarnates in the female the receptive element of force, and in the male the active or spontaneous element.[22] From then on, the free man's relation to himself as self-determination will concern sexuality in three ways: in the simple form of a 'Dietetics' of pleasures, one governs oneself in order to be capable of actively governing one's body; in the composed form of a domestic 'Economics', one governs oneself in order to be capable of governing one's wife, who in turn may attain a good receptivity; in the doubled form of an 'Erotics' of boys, one governs oneself in order that the boy also learns to govern himself, to be active and to resist the power of others.[33] The Greeks not only invented the relation to oneself, they linked it to sexuality, composing and doubling it within the latter's terms. In short, the Greeks laid the foundation for an encounter between the relation to oneself and sexuality.

The redistribution or reorganization takes place all on its

own, or at least over a long period. For the relation to oneself will not remain the withdrawn and reserved zone of the free man, a zone independent of any 'institutional and social system'. The relation to oneself will be understood in terms of power-relations and relations of knowledge. It will be reintegrated into these systems from which it was originally derived. The individual is coded or recoded within a 'moral' knowledge, and above all he becomes the stake in a power struggle and is diagrammatized.

The fold therefore seems unfolded, and the subjectivation of the free man is transformed into subjection: on the one hand it involves being 'subject to someone else by control and dependence', with all the processes of individuation and modulation which power installs, acting on the daily life and the interiority of those it calls its subjects; on the other it makes the subject 'tied to his own identity by a conscience or self-knowledge', through all the techniques of moral and human sciences that go to make up a knowledge of the subject.[24] Simultaneously, sexuality becomes organized around certain focal points of power, gives rise to a 'scientia sexualis', and is integrated into an agency of 'power-knowledge', namely Sex (here Foucault returns to the analysis given in *The History of Sexuality*).

Must we conclude from this that the new dimension hollowed out by the Greeks disappears, and falls back on the two axes of knowledge and power? In that case we could go back to the Greeks and find a relation to oneself based on free individuality. But this is obviously not the case. There will always be a relation to oneself which resists codes and powers; the relation to onself is even one of the origins of these points of resistance which we have already discussed. For example, it would be wrong to reduce Christian moralities to their attempts at codification, and the pastoral power which they invoke, without also taking into account the 'spiritual and ascetic movements' or subjectivation that continued to develop before the Reformation (there are collective subjectivations).[25] It is not even enough to say that the latter resist the former; for there is a perpetual communication between them, whether in terms of struggle or of composition. What must be stated, then, is that subjectivation, the relation to oneself, continues to create itself, but by transforming itself and changing its nature to the point where the Greek mode is a distant memory. Recuperated by power-relations and relations of knowledge, the relation to oneself is continually reborn, elsewhere and otherwise.

The most general formula of the relation to oneself is the affect of self by self, or folded force. Subjectivation is created by folding. Only, there are four foldings, four folds of subjectivation, like the rivers of the inferno. The first concerns the material part of ourselves which is to be surrounded and enfolded: for the Greeks this was the body and its pleasures, the 'aphrodisia'; but for Christians this will be the flesh and its desires, desire itself, a completely different substantial modality. The second, properly speaking, is the fold of the relation between forces; for it is always according to a particular rule that the relation between forces is bent back in order to become a relation to oneself, though it certainly makes a difference whether or not the rule in question is natural, divine, rational, or aesthetic, and so on. The third is the fold of knowledge, or the fold of truth in so far as it constitutes the relation of truth to our being, and of our being to truth, which will serve as the formal condition for any kind of knowledge: a subjectivation of knowledge that is always different, whether in the Greeks and the Christians, or in Plato, Descartes, or Kant. The fourth is the fold of the outside itself, the ultimate fold: it is this that constitutes what Blanchot called an 'interiority of expectation' from which the subject, in different ways, hopes for immortality, eternity, salvation, freedom or death or detachment. These four folds are like the final or formal cause, the acting or material cause of subjectivity or interiority as a relation to oneself.[26] These folds are eminently variable, and moreover have different rhythms whose variations constitute irreducible modes of subjectivation. They operate 'beneath the codes and rules' of knowledge and power and are apt to unfold and merge with them, but not without new foldings being created in the process.

On each occasion the relation to oneself is destined to encounter sexuality, according to a modality that corresponds to the mode of subjectivation. This is because the spontaneity and receptivity of force will no longer be distributed on the basis of an active and a passive role, as it was for the Greeks, but rather as in the completely different case of the Christians, on the basis of a bisexual structure. From the viewpoint of a general confrontation, what variations exist between the Greek sense of the body and the pleasures, and the Christian sense of flesh and desire? Can it be that Plato remains at the level of the body and the pleasures to be found in the first folds, but is already beginning to raise himself to the level of Desire to be found in the third fold, by folding truth back into the lover, and is consequently isolating a new process of subjectivation that leads to a 'desiring subject' (and no longer to a subject of pleasures)?[27]

And what can we ultimately say about our own contemporary modes and our modern relation to oneself? *What are our four folds?* If it is true that power increasingly informs our daily lives, our interiority and our individuality; if it has become individualizing; if it is true that knowledge itself has become increasingly individuated, forming the hermeneutics and codification of the desiring subject, what remains for our subjectivity? There never 'remains' anything of the subject, since he is to be created on each occasion, like a focal point of resistance, on the basis of the folds which subjectivize knowledge and bend each power. Perhaps modern subjectivity rediscovers the body and its pleasures, as opposed to a desire that has become too subjugated by Law? Yet this is not a return to the Greeks, since there never is a return.[28] The struggle for a modern subjectivity passes through a resistance to the two present forms of subjection, the one consisting of individualizing ourselves on the basis of constraints of power, the other of attracting each individual to a known and recognized identity, fixed once and for all. The struggle for subjectivity presents itself, therefore, as the right to difference, variation and metamorphosis.[29] (Here we are multiplying the questions, since we are touching on the unpublished manuscript of *Les aveux de la chair* [the projected fourth volume of *The History of Sexuality*], and beyond, into Foucault's very last topics of research.)

In *The Use of Pleasure*, Foucault does not discover the subject. In fact he had already defined it as a derivative, a function derived from the statement. But by defining it now as a derivative of the outside, conditioned by the fold, he draws it out fully and gives it an irreducible dimension. So we have the basis for a reply to the most general question: How can we name this new dimension, this relation to oneself that is neither knowledge nor power? Is the affect of self by self pleasure, or desire? Or do we call it 'individual conduct', the conduct of pleasure or desire? We shall find the exact term only if we note the limits which this third dimension assumes over long periods of time. The appearance of a folding of the outside can seem unique to Western development. Perhaps the Orient does not present such a phenomenon, and the line of the outside continues to float across a stifling hollowness: in that case asceticism would be a culture of annihilation or an effort to breathe in such a void, without any particular production of subjectivity.[30]

The conditions for a bending of forces seem to arise with the agonistic relationship between free men: that is, with the Greeks. It is here that force folds back on itself in relation with the other force. But even if we made the Greeks the origin of the process of subjectivation, it still occupies a long period of time in the run-up to the present day. This chronology is all the more remarkable given that Foucault examined the diagrams of power as places of mutation, and the archives of knowledge, over short periods of time.[31] If we ask why *The Use of Pleasure* suddenly introduces a long period of time, perhaps the simplest reason is that we have all too quickly forgotten the old powers that are no longer exercised, and the old sciences that are no longer useful, but in moral matters we are still weighed down with old beliefs which we no longer even believe, and we continue to produce ourselves as a subject on the basis of old modes which do not correspond to our problems. This is what led the film director Antonioni to say that we are sick with Eros . . . Everything takes place as if the modes of subjectivation had a long life, and we continue to play at being Greeks or Christians, and to indulge in a taste for trips down memory lane.

But there is a deeper positive reason. The folding or doubling is itself a Memory: the 'absolute memory' or memory of the outside, beyond the brief memory inscribed in strata and archives, beyond the relics remaining in the diagrams. The aesthetic life of the Greeks had already essentially prompted a memory of the future, and very quickly the processes of subjectivation were accompanied by writings that were real memories, 'hypomnemata'.[32] Memory is the real name of the relation to oneself, or the affect on self by self. According to Kant, time was the form in which the mind affected itself, just as space was the form in which the mind was affected by something else: time was therefore 'auto-affection' and made up the essential structure of subjectivity.[33] But time as subject, or rather subjectivation, is called memory. Not that brief memory that comes afterwards and is the opposite of forgetting, but the 'absolute memory' which doubles the present and the outside and is one with forgetting, since it is itself endlessly forgotten and reconstituted: its fold, in fact, merges with the unfolding, because the latter remains present within the former as the thing that is folded. Only forgetting (the unfolding) recovers what is folded in memory (and in the fold itself).

There is a final rediscovery of Heidegger by Foucault. Memory is contrasted not with forgetting but with the forgetting of forgetting, which dissolves us into the outside and constitutes death. On the other hand, as long as the outside is folded an inside is coextensive with it, as memory is coextensive with forgetting. It is this coextensive nature which is life, a long period of time. Time becomes a subject because it is the folding of the outside and, as such, forces every present into forgetting, but preserves the whole of the past within memory: forgetting is the impossibility of return, and memory is the necessity of renewal. For a long time Foucault thought of the outside as being an ultimate spatiality that was deeper than time; but in his late works he offers the possibility once more of putting time on the outside and thinking of the outside as being time, conditioned by the fold.[34]

It is on this point that the necessary confrontation between Foucault and Heidegger takes place: the 'fold' has continued to haunt the work of Foucault, but finds its true dimension in his last research. In what ways is he similar to and different from Heidegger? We can evaluate them only by taking as our point of departure Foucault's break with phenomenology in the 'vulgar' sense of the term: with intentionality. The idea that consciousness is directed towards the thing and gains significance in the world is precisely what Foucault refuses to believe. In fact intentionality is created in order to surpass any psychologism or naturalism, but it invents a new psychologism and a new naturalism to the point where, as Merleau-Ponty himself said, it can hardly be distinguished from a 'learning' process. It restores the psychologism that synthesizes consciousness and significations, a naturalism of the 'savage experience' and of the thing, of the aimless existence of the thing in the world.

This gives rise to Foucault's double challenge. Certainly, as long as we remain on the level of words and phrases we can believe in an intentionality through which consciousness is directed towards something and gains significance (as something significant); as long as we remain on the level of things and states of things we can believe in a 'savage' experience that lets the thing wander aimlessly through consciousness. But if phenomenology 'places things in parenthesis', as it claims to do, this ought to push it beyond words and phrases towards *statements*, and beyond things and states of things towards *visibilities*. But statements are not directed towards anything, since they are not related to a thing any more than they express a subject but refer only to a language, a language-being, that gives them unique subjects and objects that satisfy particular conditions as immanent variables. And visibilities are not deployed in a savage world already opened up to a primitive (pre-predicative) consciousness, but refer only to a light, a light-being, which gives them forms, pro-portions and perspectives that are immanent in the proper sense – that is, free of any intentional gaze.[35] Neither language nor light will be examined in the areas that relate them to one another (designation, signification, the signifying process of language; a physical environment, a tangible or intelligible world) but rather in the irreducible dimension that gives both of them as separate and self-sufficient entities: 'there is' light, and 'there is' language. All intentionality collapses in the gap that opens up between these two monads, or in the 'non-relation' between seeing and speaking.

This is Foucault's major achievement: the conversion of phenomenology into epistemology. For seeing and speaking means knowing [*savoir*], but we do not see what we speak about, nor do we speak about what we see; and when we see a pipe we shall always say (in one way or another): 'this is not a pipe', as though intentionality denied itself, and collapsed into itself. Everything is knowledge, and this is the first reason why there is no 'savage experience': there is nothing beneath or prior to knowledge. But knowledge is irreducibly double, since it involves speaking and seeing, language and light, which is the reason why there is no intentionality.

But it is here that everything begins, because for its part phenomenology, in order to cast off the psychologism and

naturalism that continued to burden it, itself surpassed intentionality as the relation between consciousness and its
object (being [*l'étant* or *Seiende*]). And in Heidegger, and then
in Merleau-Ponty, the surpassing of intentionality tended
towards Being [*l'Etre* or *Sein*], the fold of Being. From intentionality to the fold, from being to Being, from
phenomenology to ontology. Heidegger's disciples taught us
to what extent ontology was inseparable from the fold, since
Being was precisely the fold which it made with being; and
that the unfolding of Being, as the inaugural gesture of the
Greeks, was not the opposite of the fold but the fold itself, the
pivotal point of the Open, the unity of the unveiling-veiling. It
was still less obvious in what way this folding of Being, the
fold of Being and being, replaced intentionality, if only to
found it. It was Merleau-Ponty who showed us how a radical,
'vertical' visibility was folded into a Self-seeing, and from that
point on made possible the horizontal relation between a
seeing and a seen.

An Outside, more distant than any exterior, is 'twisted',
'folded' and 'doubled' by an Inside that is deeper than any
interior, and alone creates the possibility of the derived relation between the interior and the exterior. It is even this
twisting which defines 'Flesh', beyond the body proper and its
objects. In brief, the intentionality of being is surpassed by the
fold of Being, Being as fold (Sartre, on the other hand, remained at the level of intentionality, because he was content
to make 'holes' in being, without reaching the fold of Being).
Intentionality is still generated in a Euclidean space that
prevents it from understanding itself, and must be surpassed
by another, 'topological', space which establishes contact between the Outside and the Inside, the most distant, the most
deep.[36]

There is no doubt that Foucault found great theoretical
inspiration in Heidegger and Merleau-Ponty for the theme
that haunted him: the fold, or doubling. But he equally found
a practical version of it in Raymond Roussel, for the latter

raised an ontological Visibility, forever twisting itself into a 'self-seeing' entity, on to a different dimension from that of the gaze or its objects.[37] We could equally link Heidegger to Jarry, to the extent that *pataphysics* presents itself precisely as a surpassing of metaphysics that is explicitly founded on the Being of the phenomenon. But if we take Jarry or Roussel in this way to be the realization of Heidegger's philosophy, does this not mean that the fold is carried off and set up in a completely different landscape, and so takes on a different meaning? We must not refuse to take Heidegger seriously, but we must rediscover the imperturbably serious side to Roussel (or Jarry). The serious ontological aspect needs a diabolical or phenomenological sense of humour.

In fact, we believe that the fold as doubling in Foucault will take on a completely new appearance while retaining its ontological import. In the first place, according to Heidegger or Merleau-Ponty, the fold of being surpasses intentionality only to found the latter in a new dimension: this is why the Visible or the Open does not give us something to see without also providing something to speak, since the fold will constitute the Self-seeing element of sight only if it also constitutes the Self-speaking element of language, to the point where it is the same world that speaks itself in language and sees itself in sight. In Heidegger and Merleau-Ponty, Light opens up a speaking no less than a seeing, as if signification haunted the visible which in turn murmured meaning.[38] This cannot be so in Foucault, for whom the light-Being refers only to visibilities, and language-Being to statements: the fold will not be able to refound an intentionality, since the latter disappears in the disjunction between the two parts of a knowledge that is never intentional.

If knowledge is constituted by two forms, how could a subject display any intentionality towards one object, since each form has its own objects and subjects?[39] Yet it must be able to ascribe a relation to the two forms which emerges from their 'non-relation'. Knowledge is Being, the first figure of

Being, but Being lies between two forms. Is this not precisely what Heidegger called the 'between-two' or Merleau-Ponty termed the 'interlacing or chiasmus'? In fact, they are not at all the same thing. For Merleau-Ponty, the interlacing or between-two merges with the fold. But not for Foucault. There is an interlacing or intertwining of the visible and the articulable: it is the Platonic model of weaving that replaces intentionality. But this interlacing is in fact a stranglehold, or a battle between two implacable foes who are the forms of knowledge-Being: if you like it is an intentionality, but one that is reversible, has multiplied in both directions, and has become infinitesimal or microscopic. It is still not the fold of Being, but rather the interlacing of its two forms. It is still not a topology of the fold, but rather a strategy of the interlacing. Everything takes place as though Foucault were reproaching Heidegger and Merleau-Ponty for going too quickly. And what he finds in Roussel, in a different way again in Magritte, and what he could have found in yet another sense in Jarry, is the audiovisual battle, the double capture, the noise of words that conquered the visible, the fury of things that conquered the articulable.[40] In Foucault, there has been a hallucinatory theme of Doubles and doubling that transforms any ontology.

But this double capture, which is constitutive of knowledge-Being, could not be created between two irreducible forms if the interlocking of opponents did not flow from an element that was itself informal, a pure relation between forces that emerges in the irreducible separation of forms. This is the source of the battle or the condition for its possible existence. This is the strategic domain of power, as opposed to the stratic domain of knowledge. From epistemology to strategy. This is another reason why there is no 'savage' experience, since battles imply a strategy and any experience is caught up in relations of power. This is the second figure of Being, the 'Possest', power-Being, as opposed to knowledge-Being. It is the informal forces or power-relations that set up relations 'between' the two forms of formed knowledge. The two forms of knowledge-Being are forms of exteriority, since statements are dispersed in the one and visibilities in the other; but power-Being introduces us into a different element, an unformable and unformed Outside which gives rise to forces and their changing combinations. This shows that this second figure of Being is still not the fold. It is, rather, a floating line with no contours which is the only element that makes the two forms in battle communicate. The Heraclitean element has always gone deeper in Foucault than in Heidegger, for phenomenology is ultimately too pacifying and has blessed too many things.

Foucault therefore discovers the element that comes from outside: force. Like Blanchot, Foucault will speak less of the Open than of the Outside. For force is linked to force, but to the force of the outside, such that it is the outside that 'explains' the exteriority of forms, both for each one and for their mutual relation. This accounts for the importance of Foucault's declaration that Heidegger always fascinated him, but that he could understand him only by way of Nietzsche and alongside Nietzsche (and not the other way round).[41] Heidegger is Nietzsche's potential, but not the other way round, and Nietzsche did not see his own potential fulfilled. It was necessary to recover force, in the Nietzschean sense, or power, in the very particular sense of 'will to power', to discover this outside as limit, the last point before Being folds. Heidegger rushed things and folded too quickly, which was not desirable: this led to the deep ambiguity of his technical and political ontology, a technique of knowledge and a politics of power. The fold of Being can come about only at the level of the third figure: can *force* fold so as to be self-action, the affect of self by self, such that the outside in itself constitutes a coextensive inside? What the Greeks did was not a miracle. Heidegger has a Renan side to him, with his idea of the Greek light or miracle.[42] In Foucault's opinion the Greeks did a lot less, or a lot more, depending on your choice. They folded force, discovered it was something that could be folded, and only by strategy, because they invented a relation between forces based on the rivalry between free men (the government of others through self-government, and so on). But as a force among forces man does not fold the forces that compose him without the outside folding itself, and creating a Self within man. It is this fold of Being which makes up the third figure when the forms are already interlocked and battle has already been joined: from this point Being no longer forms a 'Sciest' or a 'Possest', but a 'Se-est', to the extent that the fold of the outside constitutes a Self, while the outside itself forms a coextensive inside. Only through a stratico-strategic inter-locking do we reach the ontological fold.

These three dimensions – knowledge, power and self – are irreducible, yet constantly imply one another. They are three 'ontologies'. Why does Foucault add that they are historical?[43] Because they do not set universal conditions. Knowledge-Being is determined by the two forms assumed at any moment by the visible and the articulable, and light and language in turn cannot be separated from 'the unique and limited existence' which they have in a given stratum. Power-Being is determined within relations between forces which are themselves based on particular features that vary according to each age. And the self, self-Being, is determined by the process of subjectivation: by the places crossed by the fold (the Greeks have nothing universal about them). In brief, the conditions are never more general than the conditioned element, and gain their value from their particular historical status. The conditions are therefore not 'apodictic' but prob-lematic. Given certain conditions, they do not vary historically; but they do vary *with* history. What in fact they present is the way in which the problem appears in a particu-lar historical formation: what can I know or see and articulate in such and such a condition for light and language? What can I do, what power can I claim and what resistances may I counter? What can I be, with what folds can I surround myself or how can I produce myself as a subject? On these three questions, the 'I' does not designate a universal but a set of particular positions occupied within a One speaks-One sees, One confronts, One lives.[44] No single solution can be transposed from one age to another, but we can penetrate or encroach on certain problematic fields, which means that the 'givens' of an old problem are reactivated in another. (Perhaps there still is a Greek somewhere in Foucault, revealed by a certain faith which he places in a 'problematization' of pleasures.)

Finally, it is praxis that constitutes the sole continuity between past and present, or, conversely, the way in which the present explains the past. *If Foucault's interviews form an integral part of his work*, it is because they extend the historical problematization of each of his books into the construction of the present problem, be it madness, punishment or sexuality. What are the new types of struggle, which are transversal and immediate rather than centralized and mediatized? What are the 'intellectual's' new functions, which are specific or 'particular' rather than universal? What are the new modes of subjectivation, which tend to have no identity? This is the present triple root of the questions: *What can I do, What do I know, What am I?*

The events which led up to 1968 were like the 'rehearsal' of these three questions.[45] What is our light and what is our language, that is to say, our 'truth' today? What powers must we confront, and what is our capacity for resistance, today when we can no longer be content to say that the old struggles are no longer worth anything? And do we not perhaps above all bear witness to and even participate in the 'production of a new subjectivity'? Do not the changes in capitalism find an unexpected 'encounter' in the slow emergence of a new Self as a centre of resistance? Each time there is social change, is there not a movement of subjective reconversion, with its ambiguities but also its potential? These questions may be considered more important than a reference to man's universal rights, including in the realm of pure law. In Foucault, everything is subject to variables and variation: the variables of knowledge (for example, objects and subjects as immanent variables of the statement) and the variation in the relation between forms; the variable particularities of power and the variations in the relations between forces; the variable subjectivities, and the variation of the fold or of subjectivation.

But if it is true that the conditions are no more general or constant than the conditioned element, it is none the less the conditions that interest Foucault. This is why he calls his work historical research and not the work of a historian. He does not write a history of mentalities but of the conditions governing everything that has a mental existence, namely statements and the system of language. He does not write a history of behaviour but of the conditions governing everything that has a visible existence, namely a system of light. He does not write a history of institutions but of the conditions governing their integration of different relations between forces, at the limits of a social field. He does not write a history of private life but of the conditions governing the way in which the relation to oneself constitutes a private life. He does not write a history of subjects but of processes of subjectivation, governed by the foldings operating in the ontological as much as the social field.[46] In truth, one thing haunts Foucault – thought. The question: 'What does thinking signify? What do we call thinking?' is the arrow first fired by Heidegger and then again by Foucault. He writes a history, but a history of thought as such. To think means to experiment and to problematize. Knowledge, power and the self are the triple root of a problematization of thought. In the field of knowledge as problem thinking is first of all seeing and speaking, but thinking is carried out in the space between the two, in the interstice or disjunction between seeing and speaking. On each occasion it invents the interlocking, firing an arrow from the one towards the target of the other, creating a flash of light in the midst of words, or unleashing a cry in the midst of visible things. Thinking makes both seeing and speaking attain their individual limits, such that the two are the common limit that both separates and links them.

On top of this, in the field of power as problem, thinking involves the transmission of particular features: it is a dice-throw. What the dice-throw represents is that thinking always comes from the outside (that outside which was already engulfed in the interstice or which constituted the common limit). Thinking is neither innate nor acquired. It is not the innate exercise of a faculty, but neither is it a learning process constituted in the external world. Artaud contrasted the innate and the acquired with the 'genital', the genitality of thought as such, a thought which comes from an outside that is farther away than any external world, and hence closer than any internal world. Must this outside be called Chance?[47] The dice-throw does in fact express the simplest possible power- or force-relation, the one established between particular features arrived at by chance (the numbers on the different faces).

The relations between forces, as Foucault understands them, concern not only men but the elements, the letters of the alphabet, which group either at random or according to certain laws of attraction and frequency dictated by a particular language. Chance works only in the first case; while the second case perhaps operates under conditions that are partially determined by the first, as in a Markov chain, where we have a succession of partial relinkings. This is the outside: the line that continues to link up random events in a mixture of chance and dependency. Consequently, thinking here takes on new figures: drawing out particular features; linking events; and on each occasion inventing the series that move from the neighbourhood of one particular feature to the next. There are all sorts of particular features which have all come from outside: particular features of power, caught up in the relations between forces; features of resistance, which pave the way for change; and even *savage* features which remain suspended outside, without entering into relations or allowing themselves to be integrated (only here does 'savage' take on a meaning, not as an experience but as that which cannot yet be absorbed into experience).[48]

All these determinations of thought are already original figures of the action of thought. And for a long time Foucault did not believe that thought could be anything else. How could thought invent a morality, since thought can find nothing in itself except that outside from which it comes and which resides in it as 'the unthought'? That *Fiat!* which destroys any imperative in advance.[49] However, Foucault speeds up the emergence of one strange final figure: if the outside, farther away than any external world, is also closer than any internal world, is this not a sign that thought affects itself, by revealing the outside to be its own unthought element?

> It cannot discover the unthought [. . .] without immediately bringing the unthought nearer to itself – or even, perhaps, without pushing it further away, and in any case without causing man's own being to undergo a change by that very fact, since it is deployed in the distance between them.[50]

This auto-affection, this conversion of far and near, will assume more and more importance by constructing an *inside-space* that will be completely co-present with the outside-space on the line of the fold. The problematical unthought gives way to a thinking being who problematizes himself, as an ethical subject (in Artaud this is the 'innate genital'; in Foucault it is the meeting between self and sexuality). To think is to fold, to double the outside with a coextensive inside. The general topology of thought, which had already begun 'in the neighbourhood' of the particular features, now ends up in the folding of the outside into the inside: 'in the interior of the exterior and inversely', as *Madness and Civilization* put it. We have shown how any organization (differentiation and integration) presupposed the primary topological structure of an absolute outside and inside that encourages relative intermediary exteriorities and interiorities: every inside-space is topologically in contact with the outside-space, independent of distance and on the limits of a 'living'; and this carnal or vital topology, far from showing up in space, frees a sense of time that fits the past into the inside, brings about the future in the outside, and brings the two into confrontation at the limit of the living present.[51]

Foucault is not only an archivist in the manner of Gogol[1], or a cartographer in the manner of Chekhov, but a topologist in the manner of Bely in his great novel *Petersburg*, which uses this cortical folding in order to convert outside and inside: in a second space the industry of the town and of the brain are merely the obverse of one another. It is in this way – which no longer owes anything to Heidegger – that Foucault understands the doubling or the fold. If the inside is constituted by the folding of the outside, between them there is a topological relation: the relation to oneself is homologous to the relation with the outside and the two are in contact, through the intermediary of the strata which are relatively external environments (and therefore relatively internal).

On the limit of the strata, the whole of the inside finds itself actively present on the outside. The inside condenses the past (a long period of time) in ways that are not at all continuous but instead confront it with a future that comes from outside, exchange it and re-create it. To think means to be embedded in the present-time stratum that serves as a limit: what can I see and what can I say today? But this involves thinking of the past as it is condensed in the inside, in the relation to oneself (there is a Greek in me, or a Christian, and so on). We will then think the past against the present and resist the latter, not in favour of a return but 'in favour, I hope, of a time to come' (Nietzsche), that is, by making the past active and present to the outside so that something new will finally come about, so that thinking, always, may reach thought. Thought thinks its own history (the past), but in order to free itself from what it thinks (the present) and be able finally to 'think otherwise' (the future).[52]

This is what Blanchot called 'the passion of the outside', a force that tends towards the outside only because the outside itself has become 'intimacy', 'intrusion'.[53] The three agencies of topology are at once relatively independent and constantly replacing one another. The strata have the task of continually producing levels that force something new to be seen or said. But equally the relation to the outside has the task of reassessing the forces established, while, last of all, the relation to oneself has the task of calling up and producing new modes of subjectivation. Foucault's work links up again with the great works that for us have changed what it means to think.

1. Line of the outside
2. Strategic zone
3. Strata
4. Fold (zone of subjectivation)

'I have never written anything but fictions . . .' But never has fiction produced such truth and reality. How could we narrate Foucault's great fiction? The world is made up of superimposed surfaces, archives or strata. The world is thus knowledge. But strata are crossed by a central fissure that separates on the one hand the visual scenes, and on the other the sound curves: the articulable and the visible on each stratum, the two irreducible forms of knowledge, Light and Language, two vast environments of exteriority where visibilities and statements are respectively deposited. So we are caught in a double movement. We immerse ourselves from stratum to stratum, from band to band; we cross the surfaces, scenes and curves; we follow the fissure, in order to reach an interior of the world: as Melville says, we look for a central chamber, afraid that there will be no one there and that man's soul will reveal nothing but an immense and terrifying void (who would think of looking for life among the archives?). But at the same time we try to climb above the strata in order to reach an outside, an atmospheric element, a 'non-stratified substance' that would be capable of explaining how the two forms of knowledge can embrace and intertwine on each stratum, from one edge of the fissure to the other. If not, then how could the two halves of the archive communicate, how could statements explain scenes, or scenes illustrate statements?

The informal outside is a battle, a turbulent, stormy zone where particular points and the relations of forces between these points are tossed about. Strata merely collected and solidified the visual dust and the sonic echo of the battle raging above them. But, up above, the particular features have no form and are neither bodies nor speaking persons. We enter into the domain of uncertain doubles and partial deaths, where things continually emerge and fade (Bichat's zone). This is a micropolitics. Here, says Faulkner, we no longer act like people but like two moths or feathers, deaf and blind to one another, 'in the midst of the furious and slowly dispersing clouds of dust that we fling at each other shouting Death to the bastards! Kill! Kill!'. Each atmospheric state in this zone corresponds to a diagram of forces or particular features which are taken up by relations: a strategy. If strata are of the earth, then a strategy belongs to the air or the ocean. But it is the strategy's job to be fulfilled in the stratum, just as it is the diagram's job to come to fruition in the archive, and the non-

stratified substance's job to become stratified. To be realized
in this way means becoming both integrated and different.
The informal relations between forces differentiate from one
another by creating two heterogeneous forms, that of the
curves which pass through the neighbourhood of particular
features (statements) and that of the scenes which distribute
them into figures of light (visibilities). And at the same time
the relations between forces become integrated, precisely in
the formal relations between the two, from one side to the
other of differentiation. This is because the relations between
forces ignored the fissure within the strata, which begins only
below them. They are apt to hollow out the fissure by being
actualized in the strata, but also to hop over it in both senses
of the term by becoming differentiated even as they become
integrated.

Forces always come from the outside, from an outside that
is farther away than any form of exteriority. So there are not
only particular features taken up by the relations between
forces, but particular features of resistance that are apt to
modify and overturn these relations and to change the unstable diagram. And there are even savage particular features,
not yet linked up, on the line of the outside itself, which form a
teeming mass especially just above the fissure. This is a
terrible line that shuffles all the diagrams, above the very
raging storms. It is like Melville's line, whose two ends remain
free, which envelops every boat in its complex twists and
turns, goes into horrible contortions when that moment
comes, and always runs the risk of sweeping someone away
with it; or like Michaux's line 'of a thousand aberrations' with
its growing molecular speed, which is the 'whiplash of a
furious charioteer'. But however terrible this line may be, it is
a line of life that can no longer be gauged by relations between
forces, one that carries man beyond terror. For at the place of
the fissure the line forms a Law, the 'centre of the cyclone,
where one can live and in fact where Life exists *par excellence*'.
It is as if the accelerated speeds, which last only briefly,

constituted 'a slow Being' over a longer period of time. It is like a pineal gland, constantly reconstituting itself by changing direction, tracing an inside space but coextensive with the whole line of the outside. The most distant point becomes interior, by being converted into the nearest: *life within the folds*. This is the central chamber, which one need no longer fear is empty since one fills it with oneself. Here one becomes a master of one's speed and, relatively speaking, a master of one's molecules and particular features, in this zone of subjectivation: the boat as interior of the exterior.

Appendix: On the Death of Man
and Superman

Foucault's general principle is that every form is a compound of relations between forces. Given these forces, our first question is with what forces from the outside they enter into a relation, and then what form is created as a result. These may be forces within man: the force to imagine, remember, conceive, wish, and so on. One might object that such forces already presuppose man; but in terms of form this is not true. The forces within man presuppose only places, points of industry, a region of the existent. In the same way forces within an animal (mobility, irritability, and so on) do not presuppose any determined form. One needs to know with what other forces the forces within man enter into a relation, in a given historical formation, and what form is created as a result from this compound of forces. We can already foresee that the forces within man do not necessarily contribute to the composition of a Man-form, but may be otherwise invested in another compound or form: even over a short period of time Man has not always existed, and will not exist for ever. For a Man-form to appear to be delineated, the forces within man must enter into a relation with certain very special forces from the outside.

I The 'Classical' Historical Formation

Classical thought may be recognized by the way in which it thinks of the infinite. In it every reality, in a force, 'equals' perfection, and so can be raised to infinity (the infinitely perfect), the rest being a limitation and nothing but a limitation. For example, the force to conceive can be raised to infinity, such that human understanding is merely the limitation placed on an infinite understanding. No doubt there are very different orders of infinity, but they are formed only on the basis of the limitation weighing down a particular force. The force to conceive can be raised to infinity directly, while that of imagining can achieve only an infinity of an inferior or derived order. The seventeenth century does not ignore the distinction between the infinite and the indefinite, but it makes the indefinite the lowest degree of infinity. The question of knowing whether or not the whole range can be attributed to God depends on the separation of whatever is reality in the range from whatever is limitation, that is to say from the order of infinity to which the range can be raised. The most typical seventeenth-century texts therefore concern the distinction between different orders of infinity: the infinity of grandeur and the infinity of smallness in Pascal; the infinite in itself, the infinite in its cause and the infinite between limits in Spinoza; all the infinities in Leibniz, and so on. Classical thought is certainly not serene or imperious. On the contrary, it continually loses itself in infinity; as Michel Serres says, it loses all centre and territory, agonizes over its attempts to fix the place of the finite in the midst of all the infinities, and tries to establish an order within infinity.[1]

In brief, the forces within man enter into a relation with those forces that raise things to infinity. The latter are indeed forces from the outside, since man is limited and cannot himself account for this more perfect power which passes through him. Thus the compound created from the confrontation between the forces within man, on the one hand, and the forces that raise to infinity, on the other, is not a Man-form but the God-form. One may object that God is not a compound but an absolute and unfathomable unity. This is true, but the God-form is a compound in the eyes of every seventeenth-century author. It is a compound precisely of every force that can be directly raised to infinity (sometimes understanding and will, sometimes thought and range, etc.). As for other forces which can be raised only by their cause, or between limits, they still belong to the God-form, not in essence but in consequence, to the point where we can derive from each one of them a proof of the existence of God (proofs that are cosmological, physico-teleological, and so on). Thus, in the classical historical formation, the forces within man enter into a relation with forces from the outside in such a way that the compound is a God-form, and not at all a Man-form. This is the world of infinite representation.

In the orders derived from it we must find the element that is not infinite in itself, but which none the less can be developed to an infinite degree and consequently enters into a scene, or unlimited series, or continuum that can be prolonged. This is the sign of the classical forms of science still prevalent in the eighteenth century: 'character' for living beings, 'root' for languages, money (or land) for wealth.[2] Such sciences are general, the general indicating an order of infinity. Thus there is no biology in the seventeenth century, but there is a natural history that does not form a system without organizing itself in series; there is no political economy, but there is an analysis of wealth; no philology or linguistics, but a general grammar.

Foucault will subject this triple aspect to a detailed analysis, and find it the perfect place in which to divide up statements. In accordance with this method, Foucault isolates an 'archaeological ground' in classical thought which reveals unexpected affinities, but also breaks relations that are too predictable. This avoids making Lamarck into a precursor of Darwin, for example: for it is true that Lamarck's genius lay in injecting a historicity into living beings in several different ways; this is something still done from the viewpoint of the animal series, to save this idea of series which is threatened by new factors. Therefore, Lamarck differs from Darwin in belonging to the classical 'ground'.[3] What defines this ground and constitutes this great family of so-called classical statements, functionally, is this continual development towards infinity, formation of continuums, and unveiling of scenes: the continual need to unfold and 'explain'. What is God, if not the universal explanation and supreme unveiling? The *unfold* appears here as a fundamental concept, or first aspect of an active thought that becomes embodied in the classical formation. This accounts for the frequency of the noun 'unfold' in Foucault. If the clinic belongs to this formation, it is because it consists in unfolding the tissues covering 'two-dimensional areas' and in developing in series the symptoms whose compositions are infinite.[4]

II The Historical Formation of the Nineteenth Century

Mutation consists in this: the forces within man enter into a relation with new forces from the outside, which are forces of finitude. These forces are Life, Labour and Language – the triple root of finitude, which will give birth to biology, political economy and linguistics. And no doubt we are used to this archaeological mutation: we often locate in Kant the source of such a revolution where the 'constituent finitude' replaces the original infinity.[5] What could be more unintelligible for the classical age than that finitude should be constituent? Foucault none the less introduces a completely new element into this scheme: while we were once told only that man becomes aware of his own finitude, under certain historically determinable causes Foucault insists on the necessity of introducing two distinct phases. The force within man must begin by confronting and seizing hold of the forces of finitude as if they were forces from outside: it is outside oneself that force must come up against finitude. Then and only then, in a second stage, does it create from this its own finitude, where its knowledge of finitude necessarily brings it to its own finitude. All this means that when the forces within man enter into a relation with forces of finitude from outside, then and only then does the set of forces compose the Man-form (and not the God-form). *Incipit Homo.*

It is here that the method for analysing statements is shown to be a microanalysis that offers two stages where we had previously seen only one.[6] The first moment consists in this: something breaks the series and fractures the continuums, which on the surface can no longer be developed. It is like the advent of a new dimension, an irreducible depth that menaces the orders of infinite representation. With Jussieu, Vicq d'Azyr and Lamarck, the co-ordination and subordination of characteristics in a plant or animal – in brief, an organizing force – imposes a division of organisms which can no longer be aligned but tend to develop each on its own (pathological anatomy accentuates this tendency by discovering an organic depth or a 'pathological volume'). With Jones, a force of fluxion alters the order of roots. With Adam Smith, a force of work (abstract work, any work that is no longer evidence of a particular quality) alters the order of wealth. Not that organization, fluxion and labour have been ignored by the classical age. But they played the role of limitations that did not prevent the corresponding qualities from being raised *to infinity*, or from being deployed to infinity, if only in law. Now, on the other hand, they disengage themselves from quality and reveal instead something that cannot be qualified or represented, death in life, pain and fatigue in work, stammering or aphasia in language. Even the land will discover its essential avarice, and get rid of its apparent order of infinity.[7]

Then everything is ready for the second stage, for a biology, a political economy, a linguistics. Things, living creatures and words need only *fold back* on this depth as a new dimension, or *fall back* on these forces of finitude. There is no longer just a force of organization in life; there are also spatio-temporal programmes of organization which are irreducible in themselves, and on the basis of which living beings are disseminated (Cuvier). There is no longer simply a force of inflection in language, but various programmes on the basis of which affixive or inflected languages are distributed and where the self-sufficiency of words and letters gives way to verbal interrelations, language itself no longer being defined by what it designates or signifies, but referring back instead to 'collective wills' (Bopp, Schlegel). There is no longer simply a force of productive work; instead there are conditions of production on the basis of which work itself falls back on capital (Ricardo) before the reverse takes place, in which capital falls back on the work extorted (Marx). Everywhere comparisons replace the general fact that was so dear to the seventeenth century: comparative anatomy, comparative philology, comparative economy. Everywhere it is the *Fold* which dominates now, to follow Foucault's terminology, and this fold is the second aspect of the active thought that becomes incarnated in nineteenth-century development. The forces within man fall or fold back on this new dimension of in-depth finitude, which then becomes the finitude of man himself. The fold, as Foucault constantly says, is what constitutes a 'thickness' as well as a 'hollow'.

In order to reach a better understanding of how the fold becomes the fundamental category, we need only examine the birth of biology. Everything we find proves Foucault's case (and could equally be found in any other discipline). When Cuvier outlines four great branches he does not define any generality larger than genre or class, but on the contrary concentrates on fractures that prevent any continuum of species from grouping in increasingly general terms. The branches or organizing elements set in motion certain axes, orientations or dynamisms on the basis of which the living element is folded in a particular way. This is why the work of Cuvier extends into the comparative embryology of Baer, based on the foldings of germinal layers. And when Geoffroy Saint-Hilaire contrasts Cuvier's organizational programmes with a single composition or structure, he still invokes a method of folding: we pass from the vertebrate to the cephalopoid, if we bring together the two parts of the vertebrate's spine, its head towards its feet, its frame up to its neck, and so on.[8] If Geoffroy belongs to the same 'archaeological ground' as Cuvier (in accordance with Foucault's method for analysing statements), this is because both invoke the fold, one seeing it as a third dimension that brings about this move under the surface. What Cuvier, Geoffroy and Baer also have in common is that they resist evolutionism. But Darwin will found natural selection on the advantage which the living creature has, in a given environment, if it makes characteristics diverge and opens up differences. It is because they fold in different ways (the tendency to diverge) that a maximum of living creatures will be able to survive in the same place. As a result, Darwin still belongs to the same ground as Cuvier, as opposed to Lamarck, to the extent that he bases his evolutionism on the impossibility of convergence and the failure to achieve a serial continuum.[9]

If the fold and the unfold animate not only Foucault's ideas but even his style, it is because they constitute an archaeology of thought. So we are perhaps less surprised to find that Foucault encounters Heidegger precisely in this area. It is more an encounter than an influence, to the extent that in Foucault the fold and the unfold have an origin, a use and a destination that are very different from Heidegger's. According to Foucault they reveal a relation between forces, where regional forces confront either forces that raise to infinity (the unfold) in such a way as to constitute a God- form, or forces of finitude (the fold) in such a way as to constitute a Man-form. It is a Nietzschean rather than Heideggerean history, a history devoted to Nietzsche, or to *life*:

> There is being only because there is life [. . .] The Experience of life is thus posited as the most general law of beings [. . .] but this ontology discloses not so much what gives beings their foundation as what bears them for an instant towards a precarious form.[10]

III Towards a Formation of the Future?

It is obvious that any form is precarious, since it depends on relations between forces and their mutations. We distort Nietzsche when we make him into the thinker who wrote about the death of God. It is Feuerbach who is the last thinker of the death of God: he shows that since God has never been anything but the unfold of man, man must fold and refold God. But for Nietzsche this is an old story, and as old stories tend to multiply their variants Nietzsche multiplies the versions of the death of God, all of them comic or humorous, as though they were variations on a given fact. But what interests him is the death of man. So long as God exists – that is, so long as the God-form functions – then man does not yet exist.

But when the Man-form appears, it does so only by already incorporating the death of man in at least three ways. First, where can man find a guarantee of identity in the absence of God?[11] Secondly, the Man-form has itself been constituted only within the folds of finitude: it places death within man (and has done so, as we have seen, less in the manner of Heidegger than in the manner of Bichat, who conceived of death in terms of a 'violent death').[12] Lastly, the forces of finitude themselves mean that man exists only through the dissemination of the various methods for organizing life, such as the dispersion of languages or the divergence in modes of production, which imply that the only 'critique of knowledge' is an 'ontology of the annihilation of beings' (not only palaeontology, but also ethnology).[13]

What does Foucault mean when he says there is no point in crying over the death of man?[14] In fact, has this form been a good one? Has it helped to enrich or even preserve the forces within man, those of living, speaking, or working? Has it saved living men from a violent death? The question that continually returns is therefore the following: if the forces within man compose a form only by entering into a relation with forms from the outside, with what new forms do they now risk entering into a relation, and what new form will emerge that is neither God nor Man? This is the correct place for the problem which Nietzsche called 'the superman'.

It is a problem where we have to content ourselves with very tentative indications if we are not to descend to the level of cartoons. Foucault, like Nietzsche, can only sketch in something embryonic and not yet functional.[15] Nietzsche said that man imprisoned life, but the superman is what frees life *within man himself*, to the benefit of another form, and so on. Foucault proffers a very peculiar piece of information: if it is true that nineteenth-century humanist linguistics was based on the dissemination of languages, as the condition for a 'demotion of language' as an object, one repercussion was none the less that literature took on a completely different function that consisted, *on the contrary*, in 'regrouping' language and emphasizing a 'being of language' beyond whatever it designates and signifies, beyond even the sounds.[16] The peculiar thing is that Foucault, in his acute analysis of modern literature, here gives language a privilege which he refuses to grant to life or labour: he believes that life and labour, despite a dispersion concomitant with that of language, did not lose the regrouping of their being.[17] It seems to us, though, that when dispersed labour and life were each able to unify themselves only by somehow breaking free from economics or biology, just as language managed to regroup itself only when literature broke free from linguistics.

Biology had to take a leap into molecular biology, or dispersed life regroup in the genetic code. Dispersed work had to regroup in third-generation machines, cybernetics and information technology. What would be the forces in play, with which the forces within man would then enter into a relation? It would no longer involve raising to infinity or finitude but an unlimited finity, thereby evoking every situation of force in which a finite number of components yields a practically unlimited diversity of combinations. It would be neither the fold nor the unfold that would constitute the active mechanism, but something like the *Superfold*, as borne out by the foldings proper to the chains of the genetic code, and the potential of silicon in third-generation machines, as well as by the contours of a sentence in modern literature, when literature 'merely turns back on itself in an endless reflexivity'.

This modern literature uncovers a 'strange language within language' and, through an unlimited number of superimposed grammatical constructions, tends towards an atypical form of expression that marks the end of language as such (here we may cite such examples as Mallarmé's book, Péguy's repetitions, Artaud's breaths, the agrammaticality of Cummings, Burroughs and his cut-ups and fold-ins, as well as Roussel's proliferations, Brisset's derivations, Dada collage, and so on). And is this unlimited finity or superfold not what Nietzsche had already designated with the name of eternal return?

The forces within man enter into a relation with forces from the outside, those of silicon which supersedes carbon, or genetic components which supersede the organism, or agrammaticalities which supersede the signifier. In each case we must study the operations of the superfold, of which the 'double helix' is the best-known example. What is the superman? It is the formal compound of the forces within man and these new forces. It is the form that results from a new relation between forces. Man tends to free life, labour and language *within himself*. The superman, in accordance with Rimbaud's formula, is the man who is even in charge of the animals (a code that can capture fragments from other codes, as in the new schemata of lateral or retrograde). It is man in charge of the very rocks, or inorganic matter (the domain of silicon). It is man in charge of the being of language (that formless, 'mute, unsignifying region where language can find its freedom' even from whatever it has to say).[18] As Foucault would say, the superman is much less than the disappearance of living men, and much more than a change of concept: it is the advent of a new form that is neither God nor man and which, it is hoped, will not prove worse than its two previous forms.

Notes

Translating Theory . . .

1. M. Foucault, 'Theatrum Philosophicum' (on G. Deleuze, *Différence et répétition* and *Logique du sens*), *Critique* 282 (1970). Translated by D. F. Bouchard in *Language, Counter-Memory, Practice*, edited by D. F. Bouchard (Oxford: Blackwell and Ithaca: Cornell University Press, 1977), pp. 165–96). Henceforth referred to as *TP*.
2. See J.-J. Lecercle, *Philosophy Through the Looking-Glass* (London: Hutchinson, 1985), p. 91. This whole book is an excellent introduction to and use of the work of Deleuze.
3. See in particular *Empirisme et subjectivité* (1953), *Nietzsche et la philosophie* (1962), *La philosophie critique de Kant* (1963), *Le Bergsonisme* (1966), all published by Presses Universitaires de France; and *Spinoza et le problème de l'expression* (1968), published by Les Editions de Minuit.
4. 'Intellectuals and Power', in *Language, Counter-Memory, Practice*, pp. 205–17. Henceforth referred to as *IP*.
5. Preface by M. Foucault to G. Deleuze and F. Guattari, *Anti-Oedipus: Capitalism and Schizophrenia* (Minneapolis: University of Minnesota Press, 1983 and London: Athlone, 1984), pp. xi–xiv; xiii–xiv.
6. For an extremely clear elucidation of this point, see V. Descombes, *Modern French Philosophy* (Cambridge: Cambridge University Press, 1980), pp. 152–6.

From the Archive to the Diagram

A New Archivist (The Archaeology of Knowledge)

1. After the publication of *MC* [*OT*], a psychoanalyst undertook a long analysis that brought out the book's similarities with *Mein Kampf*. More recently this has been taken up again by those who are opposed to Foucault and uphold the rights of man.
2. *AS*, p. 114 [*AK*, p. 86].
3. *AK*, Part IV, chapters 3 and 4. Foucault remarks that in *Madness and Civilization* he concentrated on three formations taking place on the same level: Natural History, the Analysis of Wealth, and General Grammar; but that he could have examined other formations (biblical criticism, rhetoric, history . . .) which would reveal 'an interdiscursive network that was not identical with the first, but which would overlap at certain points' (*AS*, p. 208 [*AK*, p. 159]).
4. *AS*, p. 157 [*AK*, p. 119].
5. *AS*, p. 188 [*AK*, p. 144] (and on the statement-curve assimilation, see *AS*, p. 109 [*AK*, p. 82]).
6. *AS*, p. 207 [*AK*, p. 159] (especially the critique of the *Weltanschauung*).
7. See W. Labov, *Sociolinguistique* (Paris: Minuit), pp. 262–5 [W. Labov, *Sociolinguistic Patterns* (Philadelphia: University of Pennsylvania Press, 1972 and Oxford: Blackwell, 1978). Labov's essential idea involves the existence of rules devoid of any constant or homogeneity. Another example we can give which is closer to Freud's late phase is that of Krafft-Ebing. In his enormous compilation of sexual perversions, *Psychopathia Sexualis*, his German phrases revert to Latin as soon as the object of the statement becomes too crude. There is a continual movement from one system to the other in both senses. You could say that this is because of circumstances or extrinsic variables (modesty, censorship). This is true from the viewpoint of the phrase. But from the viewpoint of the statement, Krafft-Ebing's statements on sexuality are inseparable from a variation that is absolutely inherent. It would not be difficult to show that this is the case with every statement.
8. *AS*, p. 48 [*AK*, p. 34] (the example given is that of medical statements in the nineteenth century).

9. *QA*, p. 83 [*WA*, p. 124]. And *AS*, pp. 121–6 [*AK*, pp. 92–6] (especially the example of scientific statements).

10. This explains the opening of *OD* [*TDL*]. Foucault presents 'one speaks' in *MC* [*OT*] as the 'being of language', and in *AS* [*AK*] as the statement: 'there is language'. See Blanchot's writings on 'he' (especially *La part du feu*, Paris: Gallimard, 1949, p. 29 ['Kafka and Literature' in *The Sirens' Song*, selected essays by M. Blanchot, edited and with an introduction by G. Josipovici, trans. A. Rabinovitch, Brighton: Harvester, 1982, pp. 30–42; p. 38]) and 'one' (especially *L'Espace littéraire*, Paris: Gallimard, 1955, pp. 160–1 [*The Space of Literature*, trans. A. Smock, Lincoln: University of Nebraska Press, 1983).

11. J.-P. Sartre, *L'Imaginaire: psychologie phénoménologique de l'imagination* (Paris: Gallimard, 1940), pp. 322–3 (*The Psychology of Imagination*, trans. B. Frechtman (London: Rider, 1949)].

12. *AS*, p. 118 [*AK*, p. 89] (The golden mountain . . .).

13. On 'preconceptual schemata', see *AS*, pp. 80–1 [*AK*, pp. 60–1]. On the example of the various forms of madness and the redefining of their boundaries in the seventeenth century, see *HF*, Part II [*MAC*, p. 117 *et seq.*], and on the emergence of monomania in the nineteenth century, see *MPR* [*IPR*].

14. *AS*, p. 214 [*AK*, pp. 163–4] (and *AS*, pp. 62–3 [*AK*, p. 46]).

15. *AS*, p. 138 [*AK*, p. 105].

16. *HF*, pp. 417–18 [*MAC*, p. 223].

17. *AS*, p. 210, [*AK*, p. 160].

18. *AS*, p. 129 [*AK*, p. 98] (impugnment of context).

19. *AS*, pp. 114–17 [*AK*, pp. 86–9] and *AS*, p. 109 [*AK*, p. 82].

20. *AS*, p. 115 [*AK*, p. 87] and *AS*, pp. 259–66 [*AK*, pp. 199–203].

21. *AS*, p. 143 [*AK*, p. 109]. For example, the history of philosophy as seen by Guéroult consists in sticking to this simple inscription, which is not visible and yet not hidden, without having recourse either to formalization or to interpretation.

22. *AS*, p. 146 [*AK*, pp. 111–12].

23. F. Ewald, 'Anatomie et corps politiques', *Critique*, No. 343 (December 1975): 1229–30.

24. See *VS*, 'L'incitation aux discours' [*HS*]. In fact, it is with *SP* [*DP*] that the criterion begins to be studied for its own sake. But it could be used before this, without petitio principii.

25. *AS*, pp. 145–8 [*AK*, pp. 110–13].

26. *AS*, p. 234 [*AK*, p. 179].
27. *Translator's note:* the English 'knowledge' normally translates both the French 'connaissance' and 'savoir'. Here I have had to make the distinction plain. For further clarification, see *AK*, p. 15, note 2.
28. *AS*, p. 240 [*AK*, p. 184].
29. *AS*, pp. 251–5 [*AK*, pp. 192–5].
30. *AS*, pp. 15–16 [*AK*, pp. 7–8].
31. *AS*, p. 22 [*AK*, p. 12].
32. This involves two problems, a practical one which consists in knowing where the divisions are to occur in specific cases, and a theoretical one, on which the first depends and which concerns the whole concept of division itself (in this Foucault's serial conception must be set against Althusser's structural conception).
33. P. Boulez, *Relevés d'apprenti* (Paris: Seuil, 1966), p. 372.

A New Cartographer (Discipline and Punish)

1. *SP*, pp. 31–3 [*DP*, pp. 26–9].
2. *SP*, pp. 215–17 [*DP*, pp. 213–16].
3. *SP*, pp. 223, 249, 251 [*DP*, pp. 221–2, 246, 247].
4. *VS*, p. 124 [*HS*, p. 94].
5. *SP*, p. 148 [*DP*, p. 147]. No doubt the pyramidal figure subsists, but with a function that is diffuse and spread over all its surfaces.
6. *VHI*, pp. 22–6 [*LIM*, pp. 82–6].
7. See the afterword by M. Foucault, 'The Subject and Power', in H. L. Dreyfus and P. Rabinow, *Michel Foucault: Beyond Structuralism and Hermeneutics* (Brighton: Harvester and Chicago: University of Chicago Press, 1982), pp. 208–26; p. 220.
8. *SP*, p. 196 [*DP*, p. 194].
9. *SP*, pp. 84, 278 [*DP*, pp. 82, 273]. In an interview in *Le Monde*, 21 February 1975, Foucault stated: 'Illegalism is not an accident, or a more or less inevitable imperfection ... At a pinch, I'd say that a law is not made in order to forbid any particular kind of behaviour, but in order to distinguish between the different ways of getting around the law itself.'
10. *VS*, pp. 114–20, 135 [*HS*, pp. 86–91]. Foucault never took part in the cult of the 'Law State', and in his opinion a legalistic

system is no better than a repressive one. Both uphold the same concept of power: in the one, law appears only as an external reaction to desire; in the other, it appears as a condition internal to desire.

11. *AS*, pp. 212–13 [*AK*, pp. 162–3].
12. *SP*, p. 259 [*DP*, p. 255]. See *DP*, Part 2, chapter 1 (on the penal reform movement and its statements) and chapter 2 (on how prison is not part of this system and refers to other models).
13. For a description of the Panopticon, see *DP*, Part 3, chapter 3.
14. *AS*, p. 214 [*AK*, p. 163].
15. On the development and transformation of offences, see *SP*, pp. 77–80 [*DP*, pp. 75–7].
16. See *DP*, Part 4, chapters 1 and 2 for a description of how prison further imposes itself at a second stage, in which it enters into correlation with the penal system in order to 'produce' delinquency or constitute 'delinquency' as an object (*SP*, p. 282 [*DP*, p. 277]).
17. These details are all the more necessary since *HS* will later discover another pure 'matter-function' couple: this time the particular multiplicity is numerous, in open space, and its function no longer involves imposing a conduct, but only 'administering life'. *HS* confronts these two couples on pp. 139–40; we shall return to this point.
18. *SP*, p. 207 [*DP*, p. 205]. On this point Foucault stresses that the Panopticon had a single unsatisfactory definition as long as it was viewed only as an 'architectural and optical system'.
19. On the confrontation between these two types, see *VS*, pp. 178–9 [*HS*, pp. 135–6]; and on the exemplary confrontation between leprosy and plague, see *SP*, pp. 197–201 [*DP*, pp. 195–200].
20. *SP*, p. 219 [*DP*, p. 217].
21. *SP*, p. 208 [*DP*, pp. 206–7].
22. *VS*, p. 122 [*HS*, p. 93]: 'Power is everywhere; not because it embraces everything, but because it comes from everywhere.'
23. On those integrating factors, notably the State, which do not explain power but take for granted its relations, which they are content to redirect or stabilize, see *VS*, pp. 122–4 [*HS*, pp. 93–4] and the text by Foucault in *Libération*, 30 June 1984.
24. On power-relations as 'internal conditions of differentiations', see *VS*, p. 124 [*HS*, p. 94]. The idea that the realization of

something virtual is in fact always a differentiation is analysed in depth by Bergson, for example.

25. *SP*, p. 276 [*DP*, p. 271].
26. *SP*, p. 32 [*DP*, p. 27].
27. See *SP*, p. 237 [*DP*, p. 235].
28. This is one of the links between Foucault and contemporary historians: on the subject of the flail, etc., Braudel says that 'the tool is a consequence and no longer a cause' (*Civilisation matérielle et capitalisme*, volume I, p. 128). On the subject of hoplitic arms, Detienne says that 'technique is in some way internal to the social and the mental'. See J.-P. Vernant, *Problèmes de la guerre en Grèce ancienne* (Paris: Ecôle des Hautes Etudes en Sciences Sociales, 1968, 1985).
29. *SP*, p. 165 [*DP*, p. 163].
30. *SP*, p. 226 [*DP*, pp. 224–5].
31. See *SP*, p. 225 [*DP*, p. 224].
32. For an essential text on this, see *SP*, p. 306 [*DP*, pp. 298–9].
33. *SP*, pp. 145–6 [*DP*, pp. 143–4]: 'Medical supervision [. . .] is inseparable from a whole series of other controls: the military control over deserters, fiscal control over commodities, administrative control over remedies, rations, disappearances, cures, deaths, simulations' (p. 144).
34. On trends in penal reform, and the reasons why prisons ceased to be a useful form, see *SP*, pp. 312–13 [*DP*, pp. 305–6].
35. *SP*, pp. 197–201 [*DP*, pp. 195–200] and *MAC*, chapter 1.
36. M. Blanchot, *L'entretien infini* (Paris: Gallimard), p. 292.
37. On the history and 'the systematic form of exteriority', see *AS*, pp. 158–61 [*AK*, pp. 120–2].
38. *SP* [*DP*] breaks off abruptly as soon as it invokes the 'distant roar of battle' ('At this point I end a book', p. 315 [*DP*, p. 308]). It is *VS* (*HS*] which discusses the theme of the 'points of resistance', pp. 126–7 [*HS*, pp. 95–6], and the subsequent texts which analyse the different kinds of struggle and their relations with the diagrams of forces (see Dreyfus and Rabinow, pp. 208–16).
39. See the interview in *Nouvelles littéraires*, 17 March 1975.

Topology: 'Thinking Otherwise'

Strata or Historical Formations: the Visible and the Articulable (Knowledge)

1. On the 'prison-form' and the ways in which it differs from its contemporary forms of expression (such as penal law), see *SP*, p. 233 [*DP*, p. 231].
2. On the way in which the 'meaning' or self-evidence of the General Hospital in Paris in the seventeenth century implied a 'social sensibility' that later disappeared, see *HF*, p. 66 [*MC*, p. 45]. On this same 'self-evident' character of the prison, see *SP*, p. 234 [*DP*, p. 232].
3. *AS*, pp. 236–55 [*AK*, pp. 181–95].
4. *Translator's note:* Les mots et les choses translates literally as 'Words and Things' but bears a different English title: *The Order of Things*.
5. *OD*, p. 51.
6. *RR*, pp. 140–1 [*DL*, pp. 108–9].
7. *VS*, pp. 29 and 49 [*HS*, pp. 20 and 35].
8. On the 'liberation' of madmen by Tuke and Pinel, see *MAC*, 'The Birth of the Asylum': madmen are submitted to a perpetual 'gaze' and 'judgement' (visibility and statement). The same goes for the 'humanization' of sentences in the eighteenth century: see *DP*, 'Generalized Punishment'. And, on the trend towards abolition of the death penalty, see *VS*, p. 181 [*HS*, p. 138]; punishment is adapted to the needs of a Power which no longer proposes in general to determine whether or not one should die, but instead to 'administer and control' life.
9. On the subject of the statement, see *AS*, pp. 121–6 [*AK*, pp. 92–6]. On the great murmur, see the beginning of *OD* [*TDL*] and the end of *QA* [*WA*].
10. For an outline of these three themes, see *OD*, pp. 48–51.
11. See *AS*, pp. 145–8 [*AK*, pp. 110–13], the essential text on the 'there is language', to which one may also add the whole of the end of *The Order of Things* (on the 'being of language' see *MC*, pp. 316–18 [*OT*, pp. 307–9], *MC*, pp. 395–7 [*OT*, p. 386–8] and even *MC*, pp. 57–9 [*OT*, pp. 42–4]).
12. *MC*, p. 397 [*OT*, p. 386]. See *MC*, pp. 313–18 [*OT*, pp. 299–307]. On the function of modern literature whereby it gathers language together, see *MC*, pp. 59 and 313 [*OT*, pp. 44 and 299] and *VHI*, pp. 28–9 [*LIM*, pp. 90–1].
13. *AS*, p. 168 [*AK*, p. 127].
14. See especially, in *Madness and Civilization*, the chapter entitled

'Aspects of Madness', where we are shown 'the half-perceptive, half-imaginary laws of a qualitative world'.

15. *RR*, p. 140 [*DL*, pp. 108–9].

16. *NC*, p. 169 [*BC*, p. 165]: 'when Corvisart hears a heart that functions badly or Laennec a voice that trembles, what they see with that gaze that secretly haunts their hearing and, beyond it, animates it, is a hypertrophy, a discharge.'

17. *MC*, p. 257 [*OT*, p. 244]; *AS*, p. 167 [*AK*, p. 127] (and on the 'form of exteriority', see *AS*, pp. 158–61 [*AK*, pp. 120–2]).

18. This is what the first edition of the *Critique of Pure Reason* calls 'the paradox of intimate meaning': see especially p. 136 in the Presses Universitaires de France edition.

19. See 'Speaking is not seeing', in M. Blanchot, *L'entretien infini* (Paris: Gallimard, 1969). This is Blanchot's most emphatic text on a theme that is present throughout his work. No doubt this text retains a special status for 'seeing' or the visual image (see p. 42 and 'Les deux versions de l'imaginaire', in *L'espace littéraire*, Paris: Gallimard, 1955, pp. 266–77 [*The Space of Literature*, trans. Ann Smock, Lincoln: University of Nebraska Press, 1982]. But this status remains ambiguous, as Blanchot himself says, because it confirms that speaking is not seeing rather than states that seeing is not speaking. The result is that Blanchot to a certain extent remains a Cartesian: the relation (or 'non-relation') he establishes is between determination and the pure undetermined element. Foucault, on the other hand, is more Kantian: his relation or non-relation is between two forms, determination and the determinable element.

20. On the 'dream' of isomorphism to be found in the clinic, see *NC*, pp. 108–17 [*BC*, pp. 107–17]; on the calligram, see *CNP*, pp. 19–25 [*TNP*, pp. 20–3].

21. See *CNP*, p. 47 [*TNP*, p. 36], where Foucault takes up Blanchot's expression, 'the non-relation'.

22. Some sections of *Discipline and Punish* place delinquency on the side of the prison. But in fact there are two delinquencies, the 'illegalism-delinquency' which refers to statements, and the 'object-delinquency' which refers to prison. What counts is that *Discipline and Punish* marks the heterogeneity between the development of penal law and the rapid rise of prison in the eighteenth century, just as firmly as *Madness and Civilization*

marked a radical heterogeneity between the rise of the asylum and the state of medicine in the seventeenth century.

23. See Foucault's preface to J. Brisset, *La grammaire logique* (Paris: Tchou, 1970), in which he compares the three different 'methods' of Roussel, Brisset and Wolfson.

24. *UP*, p. 17 [*TUP*, p. 11].

25. See *IPR* for a case of criminal monomania, something which poses a fundamental problem for psychiatry in the nineteenth century.

26. See the commentaries by Ishaghpour, especially on Marguerite Duras, in *D'une image à l'autre* (Paris: Gontier, 1981), and Blanchot's analysis of *Détruire, dit-elle* in *L'amitié*, (Paris: Gallimard, 1971), pp. 132–6. Foucault was very interested in René Allio's film of *IPR*. There was a problem concerning the relationship between the actions of Pierre Rivière and the text he had written (see Foucault's remark: 'The text does not relate the gesture, but from the one to the other there is a whole web of relations', p. 266); the film had to come to grips somehow with this problem. And in fact Allio does not simply use a voice-off but employs several different means in order to give a perceptible effect to the discrepancies or even dysfunctions between what is *seen* and what is *articulated*, the visual image and the auditory image (from the first shot, we see a tree in the deserted countryside, while we hear the noises and speeches of a common court).

27. *MC*, p. 25 [*OT*, p. 9]; *CNP*, pp. 30, 48, 50 [*TNP*, pp. 30, 48, 50]. *TNP* presents the two sorts of text, and draws out their maximum potential.

28. *RR*, pp. 147–8 [*DL*, p. 114].

29. This is why Foucault ultimately distinguishes between three sorts of works in Roussel: not only mechanical works where visibilities capture or provoke statements (for example, *La vue*) and works produced by a method, where statements provoke visibilities (for example, *Impressions d'Afrique*), but also the infinite work (*Nouvelles impressions d'Afrique*), where the statement proliferates in the parentheses of parentheses, and pursues *ad infinitum* the determination of the visible. See *DL*, chapter 7.

30. *RR*, p. 172 [*DL*, p. 135].

31. *NGH*, p. 156 [*NGH* in *LCP*, p. 156].
32. *CNP*, pp. 40–2 [*TNP*, pp. 32–4].

Strategies or the Non-stratified: the Thought of the Outside (Power)

1. See M. Foucault, 'The subject and power', in H. L. Dreyfus and P. Rabinow, *Michel Foucault: Beyond Structuralism and Hermeneutics* (Brighton: Harvester and Chicago: University of Chicago Press, 1982), p. 220.
2. *SP*, p. 165 [*DP*, p. 163].
3. *VS*, pp. 126–7 [*HS*, pp. 95–6].
4. *SP*, p. 207 [*DP*, p. 205] (and p. 229 [p. 228]: 'Is it surprising that prisons resemble factories, schools, barracks, hospitals, which all resemble prisons?').
5. *VS*, pp. 183–8 [*HS*, pp. 139–43].
6. See *VS*, pp. 122–7 [*HS*, pp. 93–6] for a fundamental discussion of these points and strategies, and their instability. On the subject of these resistances Foucault will explicitly use the language of particular points in mathematics, such as 'knots, focuses', and so on).
7. On the 'microphysics of power', see *SP*, p. 140 [*DP*, p. 139]. On the irreducibility of the 'micro', see *VS*, p. 132 [*HS*, pp. 99–100]. Here we ought to contrast Foucault's thought with Pierre Bourdieu's sociology of 'strategies', and ask in what sense the latter constitutes a microsociology. Perhaps in turn we ought to contrast both these forms of thought with Tarde's microsociology. The latter wished to examine the diffuse, infinitesimal relations which are not those of large sets or great men but are rather the tiny ideas of little men: a civil servant's flourish, a new local custom, a linguistic deviation, a visual twisting that becomes widespread. This is limited to what Foucault calls a 'corpus'. For a view very similar to that of Tarde, on the role of 'minute inventions', see *SP*, p. 222 [*DP*, p. 220].
8. See François Châtelet and Evelyne Pisier, *Les conceptions politiques du XXᵉ siècle* (Paris: Presses Universitaires de France, 1981), p. 1085.
9. *VS*, p. 130 [*HS*, p. 98] (Deleuze's emphasis).
10. *VS* p. 124 [*HS*, p. 94].
11. See Foucault's text on 'governments' in Dreyfus and Rabinow, p. 221; and on institutions, p. 222.
12. *VS* [*HS*] analyses these two forms, the sex that speaks (*VS*, p. 101) [*HS*, p. 77] and the sex of light (*VS*, p. 207) [*HS*, p. 157].

13. A Lautman, *Le problème du temps* (Paris: Hermann), pp. 41–2.

14. *AS*, p. 114 [*AK*, p. 85: unfortunately, however, Sheridan Smith has incorrectly translated this as 'governed by other laws than those of chance'].

15. On the statement, the curve or the graph, see *AS*, p. 109 [*AK*, p. 82]; on the distribution of chance or frequency, see *AS*, p. 114 [*AK*, pp. 85–6); on the difference between the keyboard and the statement, the letters on the keyboard and the letters in the statement, see *AS*, p. 114 [*AK*, p. 86]; and on 'the other thing' or the outside, see *AS*, p. 117 [*AK*, p. 89, where it is translated as 'something else']. On all these problems, Foucault's text is therefore very dense and concise.

16. *MC*, p. 27 [*OR*, p. 11] and *MC*, p. 319 [*OT*, p. 308].

17. See *VHI*, p. 16 [*LIM*, p. 80] (and on the way in which power makes us see and speak, illuminates things and forces us to speak, see pp. 15–17; p. 27).

18. See *VS*, p. 76 [*HS*, p. 57] and *VS*, p. 98 [*HS*, p. 73].

19. See Hans-Jürgen Syberberg, *Parsifal* (Paris: Cahiers du cinéma – Gallimard, 1982), p. 46. Syberberg is one of those film-makers who have particularly developed the disjunction between seeing and speaking.

20. *VS*, pp. 178–9 [*HS*, p. 136].

21. See the four categories of pastoral power in Dreyfus and Rabinow, p. 214.

22. See *SP*, p. 219 [*DP*, p. 217].

23. On the relations between forces, emergence and the non-place, see *NGH*, p. 156 [*LCP*, pp. 149–50]. On mutations that 'suddenly' decide that things are no longer perceived or expressed in the same way, see *MC*, p. 229 [*OT*, p. 217]. See also *VS*, p. 131 [*HS*, p. 99]: 'relations of power-knowledge are not static forms of distribution, they are "matrices of transformations"'.

24. See the article written in homage to Blanchot, 'La pensée du dehors', *Critique*, June 1966. The two points of contact with Blanchot are therefore exteriority (speaking and seeing) and the outside (thinking). And on the outside of forces as being a different dimension, 'another space' to that of external forms, see *CNP*, pp. 41–2 [*TNP*, pp. 33–4].

25. This is the fundamental issue in *The Order of Things*: Foucault does not at all say that life, labour and language are forces of

man which he knows constitute his own finitude. On the contrary, life, labour and language emerge *first of all* as finite forces external to man, which impose upon him a history that is not his own. It is only at a later stage that man appropriates this history for himself, and makes his own finitude into a grounding. See *MC*, pp. 380–1 [*OT*, pp. 369–70], where Foucault summarizes the two stages of this analysis.

26. See the closing sentence in *The Order of Things*. In the Appendix we offer a more detailed analysis of the death of man.

27. See *VS*, pp. 126–7 [*HS*, pp. 95–6] ('a multiplicity of points of resistance' which become integrated or stratified in order to 'make a revolution possible').

28. See Dreyfus and Rabinow, p. 211. And on the six particular features presented by contemporary forms of resistance, see pp. 211–22 (especially the 'transversality' of present struggles, an idea common to both Foucault and Félix Guattari). In Foucault, there is an echo of Mario Tronti's interpretation of Marxism (M. Tronti, *Ouvriers et capital* [Paris: Editions Bourgois, 1977]) as a 'workers'' resistance existing *prior* to the strategies of capital.

29. See *AS*, p. 246 [*AK*, pp. 188–9: 'The very possibility of the existence [of mathematics] implied that which, in all other sciences, remains dispersed throughout history [. . .] If one takes the establishment of mathematical discourse as a prototype for the birth and development of all the other sciences, one runs the risk of homogenizing all the unique forms of historicity . . .'].

30. *OD*, pp. 50–1.

31. See *VS*, p. 191 [*HS*, p. 145] (and all of *VS*, pp. 179–91 [*HS*, pp. 136–45]). On the evolution of law, which takes life (social law) as its human object rather than the person (civil law), the analysis undertaken by François Ewald cites Foucault as an authority. See F. Ewald, *L'Etat providence* (Paris: Grasset, 1900), especially pp. 24–7.

32. On the 'universal' intellectual and the 'specific' intellectual, see *L'Arc* No. 70 (the interview with Fontana). A more complete version in English is 'Truth and Power', in *Power/Knowledge*, edited by Colin Gordon (Brighton: Harvester, 1980), pp. 109–33.

33. *NC*, pp. 147–8 [*BC*, pp. 144–5: 'Bichat relativized the concept of death, bringing it down from that absolute in which it appeared as an indivisible, decisive, irrecoverable event: he volatilized it, distributed it throughout life in the form of separate, partial, progressive deaths, deaths that are so slow in occurring that they extend even beyond death itself. But from this fact he formed an essential structure of medical thought and perception: that to which life is *opposed* and to which it is *exposed*; that in relation to which it is living *opposition*, and therefore *life*; that in relation to which it is analytically *exposed*, and therefore *true* [. . .] Vitalism appears against the background of this "mortalism"'].

34. *VS*, p. 190 [*HS*, p. 144].

Foldings, or the Inside of Thought (Subjectivation)

1. *VHI*, p. 16 [*LIM*, p. 80].
2. *NC*, pp. 142–8, 155–6 [*BC*, pp. 140–6, 152–3].
3. *VHI*, p. 16 [*LIM*, p. 80]. We note that Foucault differs from two other views of infamy. The first, akin to Bataille's position, deals with lives which pass into legend or narrative by virtue of their very excess (for example the classic infamy of a Gilles de Rais, which through being 'notorious' is consequently false). In the other view, which is closer to Borges, life passes into legend because its complex procedures, detours and discontinuities can be given intelligibility only by a narrative capable of exhausting all possible eventualities, including contradictory ones (for example, the 'baroque' infamy of a Stavisky). But Foucault conceives of a third infamy, which is properly speaking an infamy of rareness, that of insignificant, obscure, simple men, who are spotlighted only for a moment by police reports or complaints. This is a conception that comes close to Chekhov.
4. *UP*, p. 14 [*TUP*, p. 8].
5. See *MC*, pp. 333–9 [*OT*, pp. 327–8] for 'the *Cogito* and the unthought'. See also *PDD*.
6. *MC*, pp. 263, 324, 328, 335 [*OT*, pp. 251, 313, 317, 324].
7. *NC*, pp. 132–3, 138, 164 [*BC*, pp. 131–6, 161].
8. *HF*, p. 22 [*MAC*, p. 11].
9. M. Blanchot, *L'Éntretien infini* (Paris: Gallimard, 1969), p. 292.
10. *MC*, p. 350 [*OT*, p. 339] (and on Kantian man as being an 'empirico-transcendental doublet', an 'empirico-critical doubling').

11. [*Translator's note*: As well as meaning 'double', 'doubling', etc.,
    La Doublure (Paris: Lemerre, 1897) is also the title of a novel
    written in Alexandrines by Roussel]. These are the constant
    themes of *RR*, especially chapter 2, where all the meanings of
    doublure are recapitulated in a discussion of Roussel's *Chiquenaude*:
    'les vers de la doublure dans la pièce de Forban talon rouge'
    (*RR*, p. 37) ('the verses of the understudy in the play of Red
    Claw the Pirate' [*DL*, p. 25]). [This gradually becomes 'les vers
    de la doublure dans la pièce du fort pantalon rouge' (*RR*, p. 38)
    ('the mole holes in the lining of the material of the strong red
    pants' [*DL*, p. 26]).
12. We must quote the whole text on Roussel and Leiris, because we
    feel it involves something that concerns Foucault's whole life:
    'From so .many things without any social standing, from so
    many fantastic civic records, [Leiris] slowly accumulates his
    own identity, as if within the folds of words there slept, with
    nightmares never completely extinguished, an absolute
    memory. These same folds Roussel parts with a studied gesture
    to find the stifling hollowness, the inexorable absence of being,
    which he disposes of imperiously to create forms without
    parentage or species' (*DL*, p. 19).
13. *UP*, p. 88 [*TUP*, p. 76].
14. See *UP*, p. 90 [*TUP*, p. 77] for the two aspects of 'differentiation'
    after the classical era.
15. *UP*, pp. 93–4 [*TUP*, pp. 80–1].
16. This accounts for a certain tone in Foucault, which distances
    him from Heidegger (no, the Greeks are not 'famous': see the
    interview with Barbedette and Scala in *Les Nouvelles*, 28 June
    1984.
17. Foucault does not directly analyse the diagram of forces or
    power relations unique to the Greeks. But he does appreciate
    what has been done in this area by contemporary historians
    such as Detienne, Vernant and Vidal-Naquet. Their originality
    lies precisely in the fact that they defined the Greek physical and
    mental space in terms of the new type of power relations. From
    this point of view, it is important to show that the 'agonistic'
    relation to which Foucault constantly alludes is an original
    function (which shows up especially in the behaviour of lovers).
18. On the constitution of a subject, or 'subjectivation', as

something irreducible to the code, see *UP*, pp. 33–7 [*TUP*, pp. 25–30]; on the sphere of aesthetic existence, see *UP*, pp. 103–5 [*TUP*, pp. 89–91]. 'Facultative rules' is a phrase taken not from Foucault but from Labov which none the less seems perfectly adequate on the level of a statement, to designate functions of internal variation that are no longer constants. Here it acquires a more general meaning, to designate regulating functions as opposed to codes.

19. *UP*, p. 73 [*TUP*, p. 62].

20. Foucault says that he had begun by writing a book on sexuality (the sequel to *HS*, in the same series); 'then I wrote a book on the notion of self and the techniques of self in which sexuality had disappeared, and I was obliged to rewrite for the third time a book in which I tried to maintain a balance between the two.' See Dreyfus and Rabinow, p. 226.

21. *UP*, pp. 61–2 [*TUP*, pp. 50–2].

22. *UP*, pp. 55–7 [*TUP*, pp. 46–7].

23. See *TUP*, Parts II, III and IV. On the 'antinomy of the boy', see *UP*, p. 243 [*TUP*, p. 221].

24. See Dreyfus and Rabinow, pp. 211–13. We can resume Foucault's different pieces of information as follows: (a) morality has two poles, the code and the mode of subjectivation, but they are in inverse proportion to one another, and the intensification of one involes the diminution of the other (*UP*, pp. 35–7 [*TUP*, pp. 28–30]); (b) subjectivation tends to pass into a code, and becomes empty or rigid to the profit of the code (this is a general theme of *SS*); (c) a new type of power appears, which assumes the task of individualizing and penetrating the interior: this is first of all the pastoral power of the Church, which is then taken over by the power of the State (see Dreyfus and Rainbow, pp. 214–15: this text by Foucault links up with *DP*'s analysis of 'individualizing and modulating power').

25. *UP*, p. 37 [*TUP*, p. 30].

26. I am systematizing the four aspects outlined by Foucault in *UP*, pp. 32–9 [*TUP*, pp. 25–32]. Foucault uses the word 'subjection' to designate the second aspect of the subject's constitution; but this word then takes on a meaning different to the one it has when the constituted subject is subjected to power-relations. The third aspect has a particular importance and allows us to

return to *OT*, which in fact showed how life, labour and
language were first and foremost an object of knowledge, before
being folded to constitute a more profound subjectivity.

27. See the chapter on Plato, Part V of *TUP*.

28. *HS* had already shown that the body and its pleasures, that is to
say a 'sexuality without sex', was the modern means of 'resisting' the agency of 'Sex', which knits desire to law (*VS*, p. 208
[*HS*, p. 157]). But as a return to the Greeks this is extremely
partial and ambiguous; for the body and its pleasures in the
Greek view was related to the agonistic relations between free
men, and hence to a 'virile society' that was unisexual and
excluded women; while we are obviously looking here for a
different type of relations that is unique to our own social field.

29. See Dreyfus and Rabinow, pp. 211–12.

30. Foucault never considered himself sufficiently competent to
treat the subject of Oriental forms of development. He
occasionally alludes to the Chinese 'art erotica' as being
different either from our 'scientia sexualis' (*HS*) or from the
aesthetic life of the Greeks (*TUP*). The question would be: is
there a Self or a process of subjectivation in Oriental techniques?

31. On the problem of long and short durations in history and their
relation to the series, see F. Braudel, *Ecrits sur l'histoire* (Paris:
Flammarion, 1977 [*On History*, trans. S. Matthews, Chicago:
University of Chicago Press, 1982]. In *AS*, pp. 15–16 [*AK*, pp.
7–8] Foucault showed how epistemological periods of time were
necessarily short.

32. See *SS*, pp. 75–84.

33. This is one of Heidegger's main themes in his interpretation of
Kant. On Foucault's late declarations in which he links himself
to Heidegger, see *Les Nouvelles*, 28 June 1984.

34. It was the themes of the Outside and of exteriority which at first
seemed to impose a primacy of space over time, as is borne out
by *MC*, p. 351 [*OT*, p. 340].

35. *RR*, pp. 136–40 [*DL*, pp. 105–8].

36. On the Fold, the interlocking or the chiasmus, the 'turning back
on itself of the visible', see M. Merleau-Ponty, *Le visible et
l'invisible* (Paris: Gallimard, 1979, 1964 [*The Visible and the Invisible*, trans. A. Lingis, Evanston: Northwestern University

Press, 1969]). And the 'work-notes' insist on the necessity of surpassing intentionally on the way with a vertical dimension that constitutes a topology (pp. 263–4). In Merleau-Ponty, this topology implies the discovery that 'flesh' is the place of such an act of return (which we already find in Heidegger, according to Didier Franck, *Heidegger et le problème de l'espace* [Paris: Minuit, 1986]). This is why we may believe that the analysis conducted by Foucault in the unpublished *Les aveux de la chair* in turn concerns the whole of the problem of the 'fold' (incarnation) when it stresses the Christian origins of flesh from the viewpoint of the history of sexuality.

37. The text of *RR*, pp. 136 and 140 [*DL*, pp. 105–6; 108] insists on this point, when the gate passes through the lens set in the pen-holder: 'An interior celebration of being [. . .] a visibility separate from being seen [although] access to it is through a glass lens or a vignette [. . .] it's [. . .] to place the act of seeing in parenthesis [. . .] a plethora of beings serenely impose themselves.'

38. According to Heidegger, the *Lichtung* is the Open not only for light and the visible, but also for the voice and sound. We find the same point in Merleau-Ponty, *op. cit.*, pp. 201–2. Foucault denies the set of these links.

39. For example, there is no single 'object' that would be madness, towards which a 'consciousness' would direct itself. But madness is seen in several different ways and articulated in still other ways, depending on the period in time and even on the different stages of a period. We do not see the same madmen, nor speak of the same illnesses. See *AS*, pp. 45–6 [*AK*, pp. 31–2].

40. It is in Brisset that Foucault finds the greatest development of the battle: 'He undertakes to restore words to the noises that gave birth to words, and to reanimate the gestures, assaults and violences of which words stand as the now silent blazon' (*GL*, XV).

41. 'My whole philosophical evolution has been determined by my reading of Heidegger. But I recognize that it is Nietzsche who brought me to him' (*Les Nouvelles*, p. 40).

42. What is interesting about E. Renan is the way the *Prière sur l'Acropole* presents the 'Greek miracle' as being essentially linked to a memory, and memory linked in turn to a no less

fundamental forgetting within a temporal structure of boredom (turning away). Zeus himself is defined by the turning back [*le repli*], giving birth to Wisdom 'having turned in on himself [*replié*], having breathed deeply'.

43. See the French edition of Dreyfus and Rabinow, *Michel Foucault, un parcours philosophique* (Paris: Gallimard, 1984), p. 332.

44. On Foucault's three 'problems', which obviously must be contrasted with Kant's three questions, see *UP*, pp. 12–19 [*TUP*, pp. 6–13]. See also Dreyfus and Rabinow, p. 216, where Foucault admires Kant for having asked not only if there is a universal subject, but also the question: 'What are we? in a precise moment of history'.

45. To read some analyses, you would think that 1968 took place in the heads of a few Parisian intellectuals. We must therefore remember that it is the product of a long chain of world events, and of a series of currents of international thought, that already linked *the emergence of new forms of struggle to the production of a new subjectivity*, if only in its critique of centralism and its qualitative claims concerning the 'quality of life'. On the level of world events we can briefly quote the experiment with self- management in Yugoslavia, the Czech Spring and its subsequent repression, the Vietnam War, the Algerian War and the question of networks, but we can also point to the signs of a 'new class' (the new working class), the emergence of farmers' or students' unions, the so-called institutional psychiatric and educational centres, and so on. On the level of currents of thought we must no doubt go back to Lukács, whose *History and Class Consciousness* was already raising questions to do with a new subjectivity; then the Frankfurt school, Italian Marxism and the first signs of 'autonomy' (Tronti); the reflection that revolved around Sartre on the question of the new working class (Gorz); the groups such as 'Socialism or Barbarism', 'Situationism', 'the Communist Way' (especially Félix Guattari and the 'micropolitics of desire'). Certain currents and events have continued to make their influence felt. After 1968, Foucault personally rediscovers the question of new forms of struggle, with GIP (Group for Information about Prisons) and the struggle for prison rights, and elaborates the 'microphysics of power' in *DP*. He is then led to think through and live out the

role of the intellectual in a very new way. Then he turns to the question of a new subjectivity, whose givens are transformed between *HS* and *TUP*, which this time is perhaps linked to American movements. On the link between the different struggles, the intellectual and subjectivity, see Foucault's analyses in Dreyfus and Rabinow, pp. 211–12. Foucault's interest in new forms of subjectivity was also surely essential.

46. See *UP*, p. 15 [*TUP*, p. 9]. The most profound study on Foucault, history and conditions, is by Paul Veyne, 'Foucault revolutionizes history', in *Comment on écrit l'histoire* (Paris: Seuil, 1971), especially on the question of 'invariants'.

47. The trinity of Nietzsche, Mallarmé and Artaud is invoked above all at the end of *OT*.

48. See *OD*, p. 37, where Foucault invokes a 'savage exteriority' and offers the example of Mendel, who dreamed up biological objects, concepts and methods that could not be assimilated by the biology of his day. This does not at all contradict the idea that there is no savage experience. It does not exist, because any experience already supposes knowledge and power-relations. Therefore for this very reason savage particular features find themselves pushed out of knowledge and power into the 'margins', so much so that science cannot recognize them. See *OD*, pp. 35–7.

49. Husserl himself invoked in thought a 'fiat' like the throw of a dice or the positions of a point in his *Ideen zu einer reinen Phänomenologie und phänomenologischen Philosophie* (1913).

50. *MC*, p. 338 [*OT*, p. 327]. See also the commentary on Husserl's phenomenology, *MC*, p. 336 [*OT*, p. 325].

51. See G. Simonden, *L'individu et sa genèse physico-biologique* (Paris: Presses Universitaires de France, 1964), pp. 258–65.

52. See *UP*, p. 15 [*TUP*, p. 9].

53. M. Blanchot, *L'entretien infini*, pp. 64–6.

Appendix: On the Death of Man and Superman

1. M. Serres, *Le système de Leibniz* (Paris: Presses Universitaires de France, 1982), pp. 648–57.

2. See *OR*, chapters 4, 5, 6.

3. *MC*, p. 243 [*OT*, pp. 230–1]. Daudin's exemplary study, *Les*

classes zoologiques et l'idée de série animale (Paris: Editions des Archives contemporaines, 1983), had shown how classification in the classical age developed according to series.

4. *NC*, pp. 119, 138 [*BC*, pp. 118, 136].

5. This theme has found its fullest expression in J. Vuillemin's book *L'héritage kantien et la révolution copernicienne*.

6. In *OT* Foucault constantly recalls the necessity of recognizing two stages, but these are not always defined in the same way: either, in a narrow sense, they are things which first receive a particular historicity, and then man appropriates this historicity for himself in the second stage (*MC*, pp. 380–1 [*OT*, pp. 370–1]); or else, in a larger sense, it is 'the configurations' which change first, followed by their 'mode of being' (*MC*, p. 233 [*OT*, p. 221]).

7. *MC*, p. 268 [*OT*, p. 258].

8. See Geoffroy Saint-Hilaire, *Principes de philosophie zoologique*, which contains the polemic with Cuvier on folding.

9. On the great 'break' brought about by Cuvier, whereby Lamarck still belongs to classical natural history while Cuvier makes possible a History of the living creature that will manifest itself in Darwin, see *MC*, pp. 287–9 [*OT*, pp. 274–6] and *MC*, p. 307 [*OT*, p. 294]; 'evolutionism is a biological theory, of which the condition of possibility was a biology without evolution – that of Cuvier').

10. *MC*, p. 291 [*OT*, p. 278]. We feel that this text, which deals with nineteenth-century biology, has much wider implications and expresses a fundamental aspect of Foucault's thought.

11. This is the point emphasized by P. Klossowski in his *Nietzsche et le cercle vicieux* (Paris: Mercure de France, 1978).

12. As we have seen, it is Bichat who breaks with the classical conception of death, as being a decisive indivisible instant (Malraux's formula, taken up again by Sartre, whereby death is that which 'transforms life into a destiny', still belongs to the classical conception). Bichat's three great innovations are to have seen death as being coextensive with life, to have made it the global result of partial deaths, and above all to have taken 'violent death' rather than 'natural death' as the model (on the reasons for this last point, see *Recherches physiologiques sur la vie et la mort* [Paris: Fortin, Masson et Cie., c. 1800, pp. 116–9). Bichat's book is the first act of a modern conception of death.

13. See *MC*, p. 291 [*OT*, p. 278].
14. See 'What is an author?' in *Language, Counter-Memory, Practice*, edited by D. F. Bouchard (Oxford: Blackwell and Ithaca: Cornell University Press, 1977), pp. 136–39.
15. *MC*, pp. 397–8 [*OT*, pp. 385–7].
16. *MC*, pp. 309, 313, 316–18, 395–7 [*OT*, pp. 296, 300, 305–6, 384–5], on the characteristics of modern literature as being 'the experience of death [. . .] unthinkable thought [. . .] repetition [. . .] finitude'.
17. On the reasons given by Foucault for this special situation in language, see *MC*, pp. 306–7 [*OT*, pp. 293–4] and *MC*, pp. 315–16 [OT, pp. 304–5].
18. *MC*, p. 395 [*OT*, p. 383]. Rimbaud's letter not only invokes language or literature, but the two other aspects: the future man is in charge not only of the new language, but also of animals and whatever is unformed (in the 'Letter to Paul Demeny' [Paris: Pléiade, 1972], p. 255).

Index

Antonioni, Michelangelo   107
Allio, René   141 n.26
Althusser, Louis   136 n.32
Artaud, Antonin   118, 131, 151
    n.47

Bachelard, Gaston   20, 51, 57
Bacon, Francis   vii
Baer, Karl Ernst von   128, 129
Bataille, Georges   145 n.3
Bely, Andrei   119
Bergson, Henri   4, 13, 83, 133
    n.3, 138 n.24
Bichat, Marie François
    Xavier   93, 95, 121, 130, 145
    n.33, 152 n.12
Blanchot, Maurice   7, 14, 43, 61,
    62, 63, 87, 96, 97, 104, 113,
    120, 135 n.10, 138 n.36, 140
    n.19, 140 n.21, 141 n.26, 143
    n.24, 145 n.9, 151 n.53
Bloomfield, Leonard   17
Bopp, Franz   128
Borges, Jorge Luis   145 n.3
Boulez, Pierre   22, 136 n.33
Bourdieu, Pierre   36, 142 n.7
Braudel, Fernand   138 n.28, 148
    n.31
Brisset, Jean-Pierre   131, 141
    n.23, 149 n.40

Burroughs, William R.   131

Cézanne, Paul   52
Châtelet, François   74, 142 n.8
Chekhov, Anton   119, 145 n.31
Corvisart, Jean-Nicolas   140
    n.16
Cummings, E. E   131
Cuvier, Georges   128, 129, 152
    n.8, 152 n.9

Darwin, Charles   10, 126, 129,
    152 n.9
Daudin, Henri   151 n.3
Defert,   24
Delaunay, Robert   52
Deleuze, Gilles   vii, viii, ix, x
Descartes, René   61, 83, 104
Descombes, Vincent   133 n.6
Détienne, Marcel   138 n.28,
    146 n.17
Duras, Marguerite   65, 141
    n.26

Ewald, François   17, 135 n.23,
    144 n.31

Faulkner, William   81, 121
Feuerbach, Ludwig
    Andreas   129

Fitzgerald, F. Scott   8
Franck, Didier   149 n.36
Freud, Sigmund   53

Goethe, Johann Wolfgang   59
Gogol, Nicoley Vasilyevich   1,
    18, 119
Gorz, André   150 n.45
Guattari, Félix vii, viii, 24, 133
    n.5, 144 n.28, 150 n.45
Guéroult, Georges   135 n.21

Harris, Zelig   17
Heidegger, Martin   59, 107–8,
    110–13, 116, 119, 129, 130,
    146 n.16, 148 n.33
Hitler, Adolf   1
Hjelmslev, Louis   47
Husserl, Edmund   13, 151
    n.49, 151 n.50
Jarry, Alfred   111, 112
Jones, William   127
Jussieu, Antoine-Laurent
    de   127

Kafka, Franz   1
Kant, Immanuel   60, 61, 68,
    83, 104, 107, 127, 133 n.3, 148
    n.33, 150 n.44
Klee, Paul   68
Klossowski, Pierre   152 n.11
Krafft-Ebing, Richard von   134
    n.7

Labov, William   5, 134 n.7, 147
    n.18
Laennec, Théophile René
    Hyacinthe   140 n.16

Lamarck, Jean Baptiste   126,
    127, 129, 152 n.9
Lautman, Albert   78, 143 n.13
Leach, Edmund   36
Lecercle, Jean-Jacques   133 n.2
Leibniz, Gottfried
    Wilhelm   125
Leiris, Michel   x, 99, 146 n.12
Lévi-Strauss, Claude   36
Lukács, Georg   150 n.45

Magritte, René   59, 62, 66, 80,
    112
Mallarmé, Stéphane   131, 151
    n.47
Malraux, André   152 n.12
Manet, Edouard   52, 58, 80
Markov, Andrei
    Andreevich   86, 117
Marx, Karl   30, 70, 128
Melville, Herman   44, 121, 122
Mendel, Gérard   151 n.48
Merleau-Ponty, Maurice   59,
    88, 108–12, 148 n.36, 149
    n.38
Michaux, Henri   122

Newton, Isaac   59
Nietzsche, Friedrich   x, 29, 70,
    86, 88, 92, 93, 113, 119, 129,
    130, 133 n.3, 149 n.41, 151
    n.47

Pascal, Blaise   125
Péguy, Charles   131
Pinel, Philippe   139 n.8
Pisier, Evelyne   142 n.8
Plato, 104–5, 148 n.27
Proust, Marcel   vii, 7, 76

Rais, Gilles de   145 n.3
Renan, Joseph Ernest   113, 149
    n.42
Ricardo, David   128
Riemann, Georg Friedrich
    Bernhard   13
Rimbaud, Arthur   132, 153
    n.18
Rolland, Romain   91
Roussel, Raymond   48, 52, 58,
    66, 67, 68, 80, 98–9, 110–11,
    112, 131, 141 n.23, 141 n.29,
    146 n.11, 146 n.12
Russell, Bertrand   80

Saint-Hilaire, E. Geoffroy   129,
    152 n.8
Sartre, Jean-Paul   8, 91, 110,
    135 n.11, 150 n.45, 152 n.12
Schlegel, Friedrich von   128
Schreber, Daniel Paul   64
Serres, Michel   125, 151 n.1
Sévigné, Marie de Rabutin-
    Chantal, Marquise de   7
Simonden, Gilbert   151 n.51
Simpson, George Gaylord   10
Smith, Adam   127

Spinoza, Benedict   x, 83, 90,
    93, 125, 133 n.3
Stavisky, Alexandre   145 n.3
Straub, Jean-Marie   64, 65
Syberberg, Hans-Jürgen   64,
    84, 143 n.19

Tarde, Gabriel   36, 142 n.7
Tronti, Mario   144 n.28, 150
    n.45
Tuke, Daniel Hack   139 n.8

Vallès, Jules   23
Velásquez, Diego Rodriguez de
    Silva   57, 80
Vernant, Jean-Pierre   146 n.17
Veyne, Paul   151 n.46
Vicq d'Azyr, Félix   127
Vidal-Naquet, Pierre   146 n.17
Virilio, Paul   42
Vuillemin, Jules   152 n.5
Webern, Anton   22, 52
Wittgenstein, Ludwig   50
Wolfson, Louis   141 n.23

Xenophon   100

Zola, Emile   91

Gilles Deleuze is a professor of philosophy at the University of Paris at Vincennes. English translations of Deleuze's work include *Kant's Critical Philosophy: The Doctrine of the Faculties*, *Cinema 1: Image/Movement* (both published by Minnesota), and *Nietzsche and Philosophy*. Deleuze has co-authored, with Félix Guattari, *Anti-Oedipus*, *A Thousand Plateaus*, and *Kafka: Toward a Minor Literature*, also available in translation from Minnesota.

Seán Hand is a lecturer in French at the University College of Wales, Aberystwyth. He received his Ph.D. in French from Oxford University and previously taught at four Oxford Colleges: Brasenose, St. Catherine's, St. John's, and Wadham. Hand translated the chapters by Julia Kristeva and Luce Irigaray in *French Feminist Thought* (1987) and several chapters from *The Kristeva Reader* (1986). He has contributed to the journal *Paragraph*, and is editor of and contributor to the journal *Romance Studies*. He is currently editing the books *The Levinas Reader* and *L'Age d'homme by Michel Leris*.

Since 1979, **Paul A. Bové** has been a professor of English at the University of Pittsburgh; he previously taught at Columbia University. He received his Ph.D. in English from the State University of New York at Binghamton. Bové has written *Intellectuals in Power* (1986) and *Destructive Poetics* (1980) and co-edited, with W.V. Spanos and D.T. O'Hara, *The Question of Textuality*. He contributes to the journals *boundary 2*, *Cultural Critique*, *SAO*, and *Social Text*.